BRANDING TO WIN

From Buyers To Believers:
A Blueprint For Building Brand Fandom

Fábio Tambosi

TABLE OF CONTENTS

PREFACE

You can't swing a cat these days without hitting a dozen marketing books claiming to unlock the next big thing. Most are packed with formulas and frameworks—proof points that validate a specific slice of the marketing landscape. But what many of them miss is the human element—the soul of the brand. And more importantly, how to *actually* create it.

Branding to Win was born out of two decades spent building global brands across sport, lifestyle, tech, and gaming—from Nike and adidas to Saucony and Nokia. In every category, on every continent, one truth has remained constant: the brands that win are the ones people *feel*. The ones that move beyond selling to spark identity, belonging, and belief.

This book is not about replacing performance marketing with warm, fuzzy storytelling. It's about the AND—balancing sharp KPIs with deep emotional connection. Because today's marketer doesn't just need to drive growth—they need to build meaning. And meaning is what turns buyers into believers.

Branding to Win challenges the traditional model of brand loyalty. It reframes marketing as a relationship, not a transaction. One rooted in psychology, driven by emotion, and supported by real-world results. You'll find case studies, practical insights, and a clear framework for building brands that endure.

If you're looking for a silver bullet, this isn't it. But if you're here to build something real—something people would fight for, rally behind, and wear on their sleeves—then welcome.

Let's build brands that win the right way.

— Fabio Tambosi

TO MY GREATEST GIFTS.
THIS BEGINS WITH
GRATITUTE.

To the one and only love of my life, Slavka — thank you for being the heart and rock of our family, my compass, and the constant force pushing me to become the best version of myself.

Your strength, belief, and unwavering love are the foundation of everything I do.

To the greatest achievement of my life — my love for Sara and Noah. You are my purpose, my light, and the purest form of inspiration I've ever known. Every page of this book, every idea and story, carries the hope that you'll always chase life with heart, courage, and curiosity.

To my parents and brothers — thank you for your endless love and support, always.

And finally, to Coach Kaplan and Scott Rombach — you saw something in me before the world did. You believed in my raw potential, in who I truly was and could become. Your belief lit a fire that still burns today.

This book is for all of you.

INTRODUCTION

Fandom First: The Hidden Power Behind Winning Brands

In 2017, I walked away from what most would call the pinnacle of a marketing career—my dream job at Nike. I didn't leave because I was lost. I left because I was hungry. Hungry for a new challenge, a new arena, a new mountain to climb. That next mountain was adidas. But before I could step into the role, I had to sit out a 12-month non-compete.

A year on the sidelines may not seem like much, but when you work in an industry that moves at the speed of culture, it's an eternity. My biggest fear wasn't losing a job—it was losing my edge. How do you stay sharp when you're forced to stand still? How do you stay relevant when you can't contribute?

That question became my obsession.

Instead of waiting for the world to move on without me, I chose to lean in—to rethink, reframe, and rebuild. I went back to my roots—Clemson University—and created a course for the Erwin Center for Brand Communications. Teaching became my proving ground. It pushed me to turn instinct into insight. To translate decades of experience across global brands into something tangible, teachable, true—-and scalable.

And somewhere between the lesson plans and lectures, it hit me:

The most powerful brands in the world don't just have customers.

They have fans.

Fandom is the ultimate differentiator. Fans don't just buy—they believe. They don't just wear a logo—they wear the story. They defend it. They spread it. They *live* it. It becomes part of their identity—and that's where the magic happens.

That realization changed everything. It gave language to what I had always felt but never fully defined: the difference between a brand that sells and a brand that shapes culture is fandom. That's the unlock. That's what turns good brands into movements. That's what creates staying power in a world where everything else can be copied.

This book was born out of that moment.

Not as a textbook. Not as a marketing how-to.

But as a manifesto for building winning brands—brands that don't just compete, but lead. Brands that create deep emotional connections. Brands that inspire loyalty, not just transactions.

I've been fortunate to help shape some of the most culturally influential brands on the planet—Nokia, Nike, adidas, Saucony, OneFootball, and currently ESL FACEIT Group. I've seen what happens when a brand becomes a belief system—and I've seen what happens when it doesn't. When a brand loses its voice. Its edge. Its place in culture.

Here's the truth:

- Your product can be copied.
- Your price can be undercut.
- Your media spend can be outmatched.
- But no one—not a single competitor—can steal your community of fans.

Because fandom isn't something you buy. It's something you build.

Fans are your advantage. Your margin. Your multiplier. That's the edge I spent a year off the court discovering. And that's what this book is here to give you.

The Shift from Marketing to Movement

Fandom isn't just the result of great branding—it's the foundation of long-term brand relevance in a world where attention is fleeting and competition is infinite. When products become interchangeable and media spend alone can't guarantee loyalty, the only true differentiator is emotional connection. The most iconic brands today don't just sell—they spark movements.

- Apple doesn't just launch products—it creates cultural moments.

- Taylor Swift doesn't just release music—she activates a global fanbase.

- Netflix didn't just air Formula 1—it helped turn it into a global obsession.

- LEGO didn't just survive the digital age—it built a thriving fan community that co-creates alongside the brand.

These brands win because they've built something people believe in—something people want to be part of. Now more than ever, fandom is not a byproduct of success. It *is* the strategy.

Let's unpack why it matters more than ever—and how your brand can build it.

CHAPTER 1
WHY DO BRANDS
NEED FANDOMS?

The Shift from Customers to Fans

In the traditional business landscape, brands refer to their audience as *customers, consumers, or users*—terms that imply a purely transactional relationship. While these descriptors are functional, they fail to capture the deeper, emotional connections that foster long-term brand loyalty and advocacy.

By contrast, consider how sports teams, entertainment franchises, and gaming communities define their audiences: *Fans, Followers, and Supporters*. These terms transcend mere transactions and signal a shared identity and emotional commitment. The shift from customers to fans is not just semantic; it is the foundation of a brand's ability to build lasting influence and revenue growth.

A customer remains engaged with a brand only until an unsatisfactory experience occurs. A fan, however, maintains their loyalty through challenges, setbacks, and even failures. This fundamental difference underscores why fandom is one of the most powerful assets a brand can cultivate.

The Unbreakable Power of Fandom

"Being a fan, of course, means having every right to insist, with indignation, that others achieve regularly what we could never execute just one time."

Defining Fandom: More Than Just Admiration

The concept of fandom extends far beyond passive admiration; it represents deep emotional investment and unwavering loyalty. The earliest recorded use of the word "fan" dates back to 1887[1], describing passionate baseball spectators in the United States. The term itself is a shortened version of "fanatic," which is defined as someone marked by *excessive enthusiasm and intense, uncritical devotion.* The Latin root, *fanaticus*, originally referred to individuals inspired or captivated by a deity—illustrating the almost religious fervor with which true fans engage with their passion.

This level of *dedication, identity, and emotional connection* is what sets fans apart from mere customers or spectators. Fans do not simply consume; they internalize and embody their devotion. They integrate their chosen interest into their personal identity, forming part of their *social and cultural fabric.*

Fandom as a Personal and Collective Identity

"Fandom is not just about liking something, it's about identity, community, and emotional fulfillment[2]."

For the most ardent followers, fandom is not just an interest—it is a defining aspect of who they are. Fans self-identify with specific communities, forming strong tribal connections around shared passions. Consider how *'Trekkies'* rally behind *Star Trek*, Little Monsters champion Lady Gaga, and Swifties mobilize in support of Taylor Swift, sometimes engaging in full-scale social media campaigns on her behalf. These self-given labels provide more than just a sense of affinity; they offer belonging, status, and community.

One of the most striking modern examples of extreme fandom occurred during Taylor Swift's Eras Tour[3] in Argentina. Hardcore Swifties camped outside the concert venue five months in

---

[1] John Krich, the book El Beisbol (1989)

[2] https://www.creativebrief.com/bite/trend/guest-trend/the-evolution-of-fandom

[3] https://www.teamlewis.com/magazine/psychology-of-fandom/

advance, simply to secure the best possible spot to experience the event. Logically, such behavior seems irrational. But fandom does not operate on logic—it thrives on emotion, devotion, and connection.

True Fans vs. Fair-Weather Supporters

What distinguishes true fans from casual supporters? Unconditional loyalty. Win or lose, in moments of triumph or despair, they remain steadfast. These dedicated individuals are not just supporters; they are stakeholders in the success of their chosen passion. Their emotional connection is so strong that their team's defeat or their favorite artist's criticism feels personal.

In contrast, fair-weather fans or "casuals" only engage when it is convenient. Bandwagon fans attach themselves to a team, artist, or brand solely based on popularity, quickly moving on when trends shift. To true fans, these individuals are not just outsiders—they represent the antithesis of real commitment. In the world of fandom, passion is not a part-time endeavor; it is an all-encompassing, lifelong commitment.

Why Fandom Matters

Fandom is not just about devotion to an artist, brand, or team—it is about belonging, identity, and community. When brands, entertainers, and organizations recognize and nurture their fans, they cultivate deep-rooted loyalty that transcends product transactions. Understanding the psychology of fandom is critical for any entity looking to build not just a customer base, but a movement.

Because in the end, a *customer buys from you.* But a *fan fights for you.*

Fandom: A Fundamental Human Instinct

"Man is by nature a social animal."— Aristotle

At its core, fandom is more than just a deep appreciation for something—it is an extension of our intrinsic need for connection and belonging. Aristotle recognized this over two thousand years ago, and it remains just as true today. Humans thrive in communities, whether in families, teams, or shared interests, finding comfort in being part of something larger than themselves.

Fandom provides that same sense of *belonging, identity, and purpose*. It reassures individuals that they are not alone in their passions, reinforcing shared values and building emotional bonds. But fandom is not just about togetherness—it is also about identity formation. Being part of a fan community is not just about who we are—it is about who we are not. The contrast between rival teams, competing brands, or differing artistic loyalties strengthens the collective identity of each fanbase, deepening their emotional connection and sense of exclusivity.

This *tribal nature of fandom* has profound implications beyond entertainment or sports—it is reshaping how businesses engage with consumers. Brands that understand and harness this psychological need are no longer just selling products; they are *building movements, affiliations, and lifelong loyalty*.

Fandom: The Evolution of Brand Loyalty

Fandom is the highest form of brand loyalty—an emotional connection that extends beyond transactions. Unlike traditional customer retention, which is often based on convenience or reliability, fandom fosters devotion akin to personal identity.

Brands like Apple, Nike, and Disney have mastered this dynamic, transforming customers into passionate advocates. These companies don't just sell products—they cultivate experiences, values, and community, making their fans feel recognized and included in something larger than a purchase.

Modern consumers seek brands that reflect their identity and aspirations. They don't just want products; they want stories, engagement, and shared purpose. This reciprocity defines fandom: fans demand more, but they also give more—becoming ambassadors, content creators, and lifelong supporters. The brands that understand this aren't just building businesses; they are building movements.

This deep emotional connection redefines the traditional customer relationship—moving beyond loyalty to something far more powerful: a sense of belonging. The most successful brands don't just retain customers; they foster communities where fans feel like family, driving unparalleled commitment and advocacy.

From Loyalty to "Family": A Different Type of Consumer

The key distinction between customers and fans lies in loyalty, but fandom extends beyond conventional brand allegiance—it fosters identity and emotional connection. While everyday brand loyalty is transactional—rooted in satisfaction and consistency—fandom operates on a deeper level, resembling the unconditional love found in family bonds.

A typical customer remains loyal until they encounter a negative experience. A fan, however, is more forgiving. Think about how we react when a family member disappoints us—we don't simply abandon them. That's the kind of loyalty fandom inspires—a relationship built on deep emotional investment, not just product performance.

This connection is reinforced by the Endowment Effect, a cognitive bias where we place higher value on things we feel ownership over. When someone becomes a fan, they don't just buy into a brand; they feel personally invested in its success. Their loyalty isn't dictated by price or convenience—it's driven by identity.

Brands like Apple and Porsche understand this well. Fans willingly pay a premium, not just for functionality, but for what the brand represents. These products become status symbols, statements of identity, and objects of desire. Consider the psychology behind purchasing an iPhone or a pair of Air Jordans—it's not just about utility; it's about belonging to a tribe, signaling commitment, and embracing an aspirational lifestyle.

Fandom transforms brand loyalty into something far more enduring. It isn't just about repeat purchases—it's about lifelong devotion.

To truly understand what fuels fandom, let's look at Maslow's Hierarchy of Needs, a framework that even though is not scientifically proven, explains how people seek connection, identity, and self-actualization. Fandom doesn't just satisfy a desire for entertainment; it fulfills core psychological needs, making it one of the most powerful forces in brand-building. Let's unpack how Maslow's principles can be leveraged to *create enduring, emotionally driven fandom.*

The Psychology of Fandom: Maslow's Hierarchy of Needs

Fandom is more than just *brand loyalty*—it is a subculture, built on shared passion, community, and identity. Fans don't just engage with a brand; they immerse themselves in its world, obsessing over details, consuming content, and forming social connections around their shared interest. This behavior isn't random—it is deeply rooted in human psychology.

To understand why fandom is so powerful, we must explore what drives it. This brings us to Abraham Maslow's Hierarchy of Needs[4], a foundational theory of human motivation. Maslow's framework is structured as a pyramid, with basic physiological needs at the bottom and higher-level psychological and self-fulfillment needs at the top. According to Maslow, individuals must satisfy lower-tier needs before advancing to higher levels of fulfillment.

Where does fandom fit within this hierarchy of needs? Primarily in the third and fourth-tiers: *Love & Belonging and Esteem.* Fans find community and connection (Love & Belonging) through shared enthusiasm, whether for a sports team, a music artist, or a gaming franchise. Fandom also reinforces self-esteem, as identification with a brand, team, or movement provides a sense of pride, status, and purpose.

In some cases, fandom can even reach the highest level—Self-Actualization—when fans feel a profound sense of meaning and personal fulfillment through their engagement. This could be seen in superfans who dedicate their lives to their passion, create content, or actively contribute to their community.

For brands, the key to building a devoted fanbase is to connect with audiences at the lower levels of the pyramid first, cultivating emotional bonds before attempting to create status-

---

[4] https://www.simplypsychology.org/maslow.html

driven or aspirational associations. Understanding these psychological drivers allows brands to move beyond transactions and build movements.

Wrexham AFC:
A Case Study in Fandom-Driven Transformation

One of the most compelling examples of how fandom can transform a brand is the remarkable story of Wrexham AFC[5], the Welsh football club revitalized by Hollywood actors Ryan Reynolds and Rob McElhenney.

Before the duo's purchase in 2020, Wrexham AFC had been relegated to near obscurity, despite boasting a rich 150-year history. Financial struggles, declining attendance, and a lack of visibility had left the club struggling in the lower leagues. However, everything changed the moment Reynolds and McElhenney took over. Their involvement instantly propelled Wrexham into the global spotlight, with millions of people following the club's journey thanks to social media buzz and the powerful storytelling behind the takeover.

The intrigue was further amplified by the critically acclaimed documentary series "Welcome to Wrexham", which chronicled the club's history, the challenges of ownership, and the emotional connection between the team and its community. This behind-the-scenes storytelling humanized the club, allowing fans worldwide to experience the highs and lows of Wrexham's journey.

The impact was immediate and profound. Sponsorship deals from major brands flooded in, home games became sellouts, and the club's merchandise sales skyrocketed. Hollywood A-listers such as Will Ferrell and Hugh Jackman were spotted in the stands, reinforcing the club's newfound mainstream appeal.

But the most important transformation happened on the pitch. Buoyed by overwhelming fan support and renewed financial investment, the team improved its performance, culminating in its historic promotion to the fully professional fourth division during the 2022/23 season— a momentous achievement for the club..

---

[5] https://www.wales.com/culture-and-sport/sport/wrexham-goes-hollywood

Caption.: Wrexham AFC supporters during the promotion parade.

Wrexham AFC's rise exemplifies the *power of fandom-driven growth*. The club didn't just gain new supporters; it built a global community of engaged, emotionally invested fans who felt part of its story. This case demonstrates how authentic engagement, compelling storytelling, and emotional connection can transform a struggling brand into a cultural phenomenon—reinforcing the idea that fandom is one of the most valuable assets a brand can cultivate.

The Business Case for Fandom

Fandom is not merely an abstract concept—it is a measurable driver of revenue, engagement, and influence. Unlike traditional consumers, fans:

- Engage deeply with content—spending hours consuming, sharing, and creating related material.
- Act as brand evangelists—advocating for and defending their chosen brand within their networks.
- Demonstrate higher lifetime value—spending more money and remaining loyal even amid challenges.

Fandom Fuels Social Currency

For Gen Z and younger Millennials, fandom is a defining aspect of identity. Social currency—the value derived from shared cultural engagement—dictates how these consumers interact with brands. This is critical for marketers because social currency drives purchasing decisions far more effectively than traditional advertising. Authenticity, community engagement, and experiential interactions now shape brand perception.

A well-cultivated fandom:

- Creates community-driven engagement that thrives independently of traditional marketing campaigns.

- Generates organic user-driven content, fueling brand awareness without requiring large advertising budgets.

- Strengthens emotional ties that make customers more likely to support a brand even during downturns.

How Social Media Transformed Fandom

Fandom has evolved dramatically in the digital age. Prior to the internet, fan communities were largely local and event-driven—concerts, sports games, and conventions were primary gathering spaces. Interaction was limited to in-person experiences and print media.

Today, social media has made fandom *borderless and interactive.* Platforms like TikTok, Twitter, Instagram, and Reddit allow fans to engage in real-time, influence conversations, and connect with global communities. The result is an unprecedented level of access and participation.

For sports fans, social media has revolutionized how they interact with teams and athletes. Players are no longer distant figures on a field or court—they are accessible, engaging, and part of a daily content ecosystem. Similarly, in entertainment and gaming, fans influence trends, content direction, and brand decisions through direct engagement. The shift is profound: fans expect two-way communication rather than passive consumption.

Additionally, fans themselves have become influencers, shaping brand narratives and driving trends. Some fan accounts amass hundreds of thousands of followers, wielding influence comparable to traditional media outlets. The power dynamic has shifted—from brands controlling messaging to fans shaping brand perception.

Esports & Gaming: The Next Frontier of Fandom

Gaming represents one of the largest and fastest-growing fandom ecosystems. With 3.2 billion global gamers and an expected 640 million esports fans by 2025, with 69% of esports fans being Gen Zs, a cohort representing $330 billion in annual spending power

Gaming and esports are no longer niche—it is mainstream entertainment.

Their fans don't just watch—they interact, compete, and shape the culture. Brands that fail to recognize gaming's role in modern fandom risk being left behind.

Esports fandom mirrors sports, music, and entertainment culture, yet it remains undervalued by traditional marketers. This audience is not passive—it is participatory, loyal, and highly engaged. Much like K-pop fans, esports fans orchestrate viral campaigns, community-driven events, and global movements.

Fandom as a Growth Lever:
A Case Study from ESL FACEIT Group

This deep-rooted sense of fandom isn't just theoretical—it's something I've experienced firsthand in my work at ESL FACEIT Group. In my role, I've seen how passionate gaming communities mirror the behaviors of sports and lifestyle brand fans, turning engagement into devotion, advocacy, and sustained growth. One particular case stands out as a testament to how fandom can be harnessed to drive both brand loyalty and commercial success.

At ESL FACEIT Group, one of the team's strategic priorities was optimizing our ticket pricing model. The prevailing concern within the product team was that increasing prices would provoke a backlash from the community, resulting in decline in sales and attendance. But, scarcity is one of the strongest tools to create pent-up demand, especially with a community of aficionados, and increase perceived value—when executed strategically, price increases can actually strengthen engagement and drive higher conversions.

To test this, the marketing team developed a tiered pricing strategy, releasing batches of limited-quantity tickets every four to six weeks. Staggering availability creates scarcity, amplifies demand, and incentivizes early purchases. The results spoke for themselves.

This resulted in increased revenue of +60% in like-for-like events versus previous year— EFG sold out every single venue across 27 events. This approach delivered record-breaking attendance unlocking unprecedented revenue growth and a healthier profit margin. In 2024, EFG's events hosted 300,000 fans attending our tournaments and festivals around the world.

This case illustrates a critical truth about fandom: when fans are emotionally invested, they see value beyond price. The key isn't just selling a ticket—it's creating an experience that feels exclusive, aspirational, and deeply connected to their identity.

How Brands Can Cultivate Fandom

Building a fandom requires moving beyond transactional marketing and embracing brand immersion, community-building, and experience-driven engagement. Brands that excel at fandom cultivation—Nike, Apple, Netflix, and adidas—understand that their role is not just to sell but to invite participation and shared identity.

Successful fan-driven brands:

- Create unique rituals that reinforce shared experiences (Nike's "Just Do It" mindset, Apple's product launches).

- Encourage community engagement by fostering discussion, collaboration, and advocacy.

- Empower fans as co-creators, letting them shape the brand experience (user-generated content, influencer collaborations).

In contrast, brands that fail to embrace fandom often struggle with low engagement, weak loyalty, and a high cost of customer acquisition.

The Neurological Power of Sports Fandom

Sports fandom is more than just passion—it is a deeply ingrained neurological and emotional experience. The intense pride, rituals, superstitions, and collective euphoria that define sports culture are not random; they are biologically rooted in human connection and identity formation.

Fans don't just watch the game—they experience it on a physiological level. Neuroscientific research shows that the neurons in a fan's brain fire in sync with the athletes they admire, mirroring their movements and emotional highs and lows. Endocrinologists have further demonstrated that fans' hormonal responses, including adrenaline and cortisol spikes, can replicate those of the players competing on the field. This explains why the agony of a missed penalty or the ecstasy of a last-minute goal feels intensely personal.

Psychologist Stephen Reysen, professor at Texas A&M, articulates this phenomenon clearly: *"Individuals feel that the fan interest (in this case a sports team) is a part of them, so when the team is winning, you feel like you are winning even though you are not a player."*[6] This connection is so profound that it shapes self-esteem, optimism, and overall well-being, making sports fandom a powerful psychological anchor in fans' lives.

Moreover, fandom serves as an emotional release, offering a socially acceptable outlet for passion, camaraderie, and even vulnerability. In a society where emotional restraint is often expected, sports provide a rare space where fans can express unfiltered joy, frustration, and connection without restraint. When their team scores the winning goal, stoic individuals erupt in celebration, embracing strangers as if they had personally delivered the victory. This is the essence of fandom—shared triumphs, communal belonging, and an unwavering emotional bond that transcends the game itself.

The Expanding Influence of Music Fandom

The evolving landscape of media consumption has transformed the way fans engage with music, shifting from passive listening to immersive, multidimensional experiences. Music fandom is no longer limited to albums, concerts, and interviews—it extends into personal, cultural, and even political spheres, deeply influencing the identities and perspectives of fans.

The graph below visualizes the depth of fan engagement, illustrating how insightful and experiential content shapes the modern music experience. Fans today are not just consumers; they are active participants in an ongoing dialogue with their favorite artists. They frequently engage with behind-the-scenes content, documentary-style storytelling, and artist-driven narratives, seeking a more intimate connection beyond the music itself.

---

[6] https://thehoya.com/sports/lonergan-its-not-just-a-game-the-psychology-of-being-a-sports-fan/

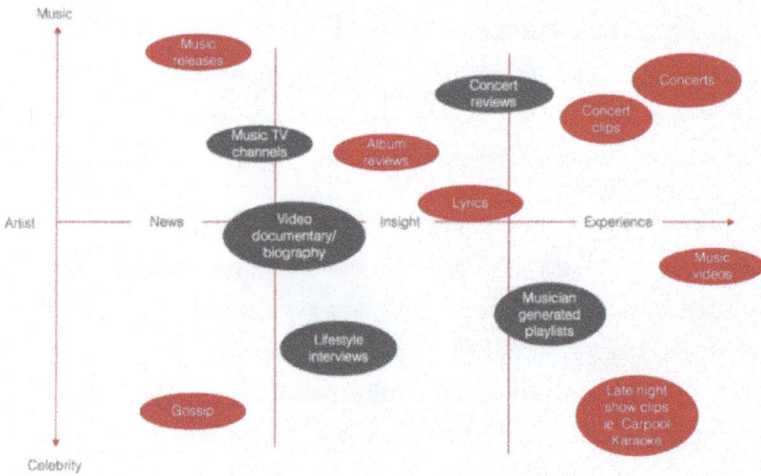

Thanks largely to social media, this interaction has broadened and deepened, creating a two-way communication channel between artists and their audiences. Platforms like Instagram, TikTok, and Twitter have dismantled traditional barriers, allowing fans to experience artists not just as performers, but as fully formed individuals with personal, spiritual, and political viewpoints. This direct access fosters a level of intimacy that was once unimaginable—fans feel a genuine emotional investment in their favorite musicians' lives.

Artists like Taylor Swift, Lady Gaga, Ed Sheeran, and Billie Eilish exemplify this shift, leveraging their platforms to engage fans beyond music, and influencing conversations around mental health, social justice, and cultural identity. These interactions elevate fandom from simple admiration to a deeply personal connection, reinforcing the idea that in the digital age, fandom is not just about entertainment—it is about belonging, shared values, and cultural influence.

Final Thought: The Cult of Fandom

Fandom is not the same as traditional brand loyalty—it is deeper, emotional, and rooted in identity. As digital connectivity reshapes consumer behavior, brands must evolve from selling products to fostering communities. Customers buy from a brand. Fans fight for it. The future of branding is not about transactions—it is about reciprocal relationships. Welcome to the era of Winning Brands.

CHAPTER 2
TURNING BUYERS INTO DEVOTED FANS

Know Your Fans

You have an audience. They are watching, waiting, and expecting something from you. But who are they, really?

Understanding your audience is not just a marketing exercise—it's the foundation of building a brand that stands the test of time. Every company has customers, and many have loyal ones. But true fans? That's an entirely different level of engagement. Fans don't just buy your product; they integrate your brand into their identity. They advocate for you, defend you, and celebrate your successes as if they were their own. They're not just consumers; they are participants in your brand's story.

This distinction between customers and fans is what separates transactional brands from cultural movements. It's what makes an Apple launch an event, a Nike sneaker release a global phenomenon, and a Starbucks order a daily ritual. Fandom is the difference between a brand that is merely liked and one that is truly loved.

But fandom doesn't happen by accident. It requires a deep understanding of who your audience is, what they value, and how your brand fits into their lives. The brands that thrive are the ones that don't just sell—they connect. They don't just attract buyers—they create believers.

So, do you really know your audience? More importantly, do you know how to turn them into fans?

This chapter will explore the psychology behind fandom, the emotional triggers that drive deep brand loyalty, and the strategic approach you need to cultivate a community of devoted followers. Because in today's world, customers may come and go—but fans are forever.

Inside the Mind of Your Fans

Fandom isn't just about liking a brand—it's about identifying with it. Just as sports fans rally behind their teams based on shared values, heritage, and emotional connection, brand fans form attachments that go far beyond the product itself. Why does one person pledge unwavering loyalty to Chelsea Football Club while another is a lifelong Liverpool supporter?

Why do Real Madrid and FC Barcelona inspire generations of devoted followers, or why do college football fans fiercely defend Clemson Tigers over Alabama Crimson Tide Football? These allegiances aren't just about geography or performance—they stem from a sense of belonging, shared identity, and personal values.

The same principle applies to brands. But before a company can expect fans to embrace its values, it must first define them with absolute clarity. A brand that lacks self-awareness will struggle to cultivate meaningful and lasting connections. This is where the concept of a **"Why" statement** comes into play—a foundational belief that drives everything a brand stands for beyond simply generating profit. It is the motivator behind avid football fans and brand consumers alike. "It's the thing that pushes people not just to buy but to believe."[7]

Simon Sinek, in his now-famous TED Talk on the "Golden Circle," emphasized the power of starting with *why* rather than just *what* a company sells. This principle doesn't just apply to business strategy; it is the very reason fans commit to a brand on an emotional level. People don't just buy products—they buy into belief systems. The same force that compels fans to stand by their team, regardless of wins or losses, fuels the most powerful brand fandoms.

The brands that build lasting, passionate fan bases aren't just selling—they're inspiring. But how do you tap into that emotional connection? The answer lies in understanding your audience on a deeper level—what they care about, what drives them, and how your brand can become a part of their identity. Let's explore how to develop this connection and turn customers into devoted fans.

---

[7] https://agencyinmotion.com/the-psychology-of-belonging/

From Transactional to Emotional:
The Fan vs. The Customer

Loyalty in business has traditionally been measured by repeat purchases, customer retention, and lifetime value. But true brand loyalty goes beyond transactions—it is emotional, not just behavioral. Fans don't just buy from a brand; they identify with it, advocate for it, and defend it as if it were part of their own personal story. The shift from customer to fan marks the difference between a brand people *use* and a brand people *love*.

This is the ultimate goal for any company: moving beyond a transactional relationship with customers and building an emotional connection that fosters deep, long-term commitment. But what drives this shift? What makes someone fall in love with a brand rather than simply shop from it? And how do brands cultivate a sense of fandom that turns casual buyers into lifelong advocates?

Few franchises exemplify the power of fandom better than *Harry Potter*. What started as a children's book series became a multi-billion-dollar global entertainment empire, driven not just by sales, but by an emotionally invested community. The devoted fan base—Potterheads—has turned *Harry Potter* into more than just a series of books or movies. It's a cultural identity, complete with self-defined houses, immersive theme parks, and an endless stream of user-generated content, from fanfiction to elaborate cosplay. The *Harry Potter* fans didn't just consume the brand—they built it. By engaging deeply with the world J.K. Rowling created, these fans extended the lifespan and profitability of the franchise far beyond its original form, proving that true fandom can be one of the most valuable assets a brand can cultivate.

To answer these questions, we need to explore the fundamental psychological and emotional triggers that differentiate fans from customers—and why fandom is the most powerful competitive advantage a brand can cultivate.

The Fundamental Difference: Fans vs. Customers

This level of connection compounds a brand's success in ways that go beyond conventional marketing metrics. Fans do not merely consume—they promote, defend, and champion the brands they love. They introduce new customers to your products, amplify your message, and actively participate in shaping the brand's evolution. Their advocacy is **authentic and unpaid**, yet it holds more influence than any traditional advertising campaign.

Unlike transactional customers, who may switch brands after a single negative experience, fans are more forgiving. When a brand stumbles—whether through a flawed product launch, a service disruption, or an external controversy—fans don't abandon ship. Instead, they rally, offer feedback, and often support the brand through its evolution. Apple's transformation of MobileMe into iCloud is a prime example: instead of losing its loyal base after a shaky product rollout, the company refined and improved its offering, with fans remaining deeply invested in the journey.

The Science of Brand Devotion: How Emotional Connection Drives Fandom

At the core of fandom lies emotional investment—a stark contrast to the transactional nature of traditional customer relationships. A customer engages with a brand based on factors like price, convenience, or necessity. Their loyalty is conditional: a better deal, a more convenient option, or a single negative experience can drive them elsewhere.

A fan, on the other hand, is not just loyal; they are emotionally tethered to the brand. They see it as an extension of themselves, integrating it into their identity and lifestyle. Their connection is not just about the product but about belonging, meaning and personal expression. They don't just consume the brand; they advocate for it, defend it, and celebrate its success as if it were their own.

This depth of attachment isn't just anecdotal—it has neurological roots. In 2005, biological anthropologist Helen Fisher[8] conducted a groundbreaking study examining the neuroscience of love. She and her research team analyzed 2,500 brain scans of individuals experiencing romantic love, using functional MRI (fMRI) technology to track neurological activity.

When participants viewed images of someone they loved, their brains lit up in regions rich with dopamine, the neurotransmitter associated with pleasure, motivation, and reward. Two key areas were activated:

- The caudate nucleus, responsible for reward detection and the expectation of positive outcomes.
- The ventral tegmental area (VTA), linked to motivation, focus, and the pursuit of rewards.

---

[8] https://hms.harvard.edu/news-events/publications-archive/brain/love-brain

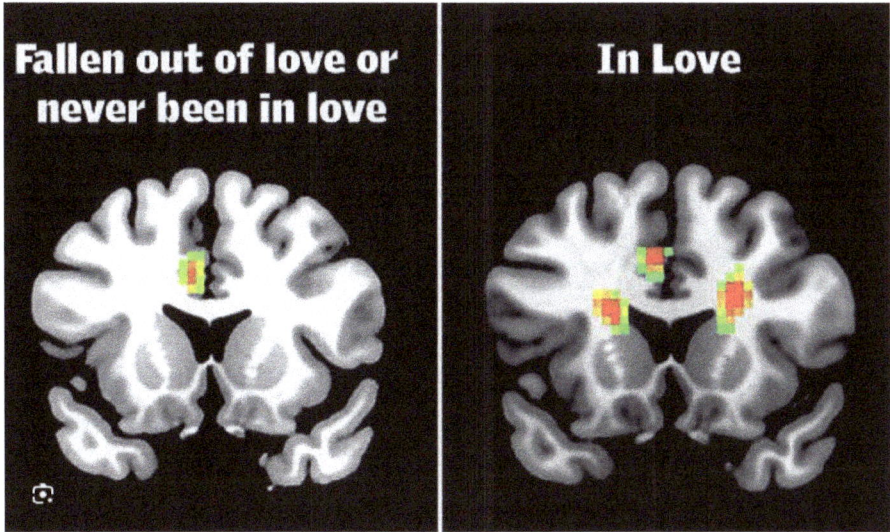

Fallen out of love or never been in love | In Love

This neurological response is strikingly similar to what happens in the brains of devoted brand fans. When a die-hard sneaker collector finally gets their hands on a limited-edition pair of Jordans, or when a passionate esports fan watches their favorite team win a championship, the same dopamine-driven reward circuits are engaged.

Fandom, then, is not just about preference—it is a biologically ingrained phenomenon. Just as love triggers a powerful neurochemical response, so too does deep emotional brand attachment. This explains why fans remain committed to a brand even in the face of competition, price changes, or product evolution.

Understanding this fundamental difference between customers and fans is the key to building a brand that is not just used, but loved. The brands that successfully create this emotional connection don't just offer products—they become part of their audience's identity.

Fandom as a Growth Engine

A fan-centric approach to branding isn't just a feel-good strategy—it's a proven business model. Research shows that loyal customers spend more, return more frequently, and have a higher lifetime value than casual buyers. Fan loyalty translates into sustained revenue, lower customer acquisition costs, and long-term market dominance.

More importantly, fandom builds brand resilience. Economic downturns, market shifts, and competitive threats impact every brand—but those with a strong fan base weather challenges more effectively. Winning Brands like Nike, Harley-Davidson, and Supreme don't just sell products; they create cultures, movements, and identities that persist across generations.

Brand Integrity: The Key to Lasting Fandom

At the heart of every thriving fandom is a foundation of trust, built not just on product quality but on brand integrity. Fans don't just buy into what a brand sells; they buy into what it stands for. The most critical element in cultivating this devotion is **congruence**—a brand's ability to align its actions with its values consistently. When a brand operates with authenticity and stays true to its purpose, it fosters a sense of reliability, credibility, and emotional investment among its audience.

But when brands fail to maintain this integrity—by making empty promises, contradicting their core values, or prioritizing profit over purpose—they risk something far more damaging than customer churn: brand infidelity. This phenomenon occurs when a brand's actions betray the trust of its fans, leading to disillusionment and, in many cases, abandonment. And once that trust is broken, even the most loyal fans may walk away.

The Power of Brand Integrity: Lessons from Apple

Apple provides a compelling case study on the long-term benefits of brand congruence and the resilience of fan loyalty. The company has consistently positioned itself as an innovator— one that challenges the status quo and empowers its users with cutting-edge design and technology. This brand identity has been so deeply ingrained in its fanbase that even when Apple has stumbled (as it did with failures like the Apple Newton and MobileMe, the precursor to iCloud), its fans remain committed. They didn't abandon Apple; instead, they engaged in discussions, provided feedback, and anticipated the next evolution of the brand.

This is the power of fandom. Unlike regular customers who might walk away after a single bad experience, fans are invested in a brand's **journey**, not just its products. They participate in shaping its future, offering constructive criticism and eagerly anticipating improvements. Their connection goes beyond mere transactions—it is deeply emotional and participatory.

Fandom as a Compound Growth Engine

Leading a brand with a **fan-centric approach** creates a compound effect on success. A community of emotionally invested fans becomes a force multiplier, amplifying a brand's reach, credibility, and longevity. This is why the most successful brands don't just focus on selling—they focus on building relationships.

Take sports fandom as an example. The love for a team isn't just about the latest season's performance; it's a legacy passed down through generations. The Chicago Cubs, for example, went over 100 years without a championship but still maintained one of the most devoted fan bases in professional sports. This is because fandom transcends performance—it is rooted in identity, culture, and tradition.

Brands that understand this principle can weather economic downturns, market shifts, and competitive threats because their fans don't abandon them at the first sign of trouble. Instead, they rally behind them, defending them in public forums, advocating for them in social circles, and remaining engaged even when products or services face temporary setbacks.

The Priceless Nature of Organic Fandom

This type of word-of-mouth advocacy is invaluable. Research consistently shows that fan loyalty leads to long-term revenue growth. According to multiple studies, loyal customers are willing to spend more on brands they love and are significantly less likely to switch to competitors—even when alternatives are cheaper or more convenient. This behavior is not driven by rational decision-making alone but by emotional connection and a sense of belonging.

A true fandom operates much like a tribe or movement—where members aren't just passive consumers but active participants in shaping the brand's identity. They expect more than just great products; they want to feel seen, heard, and valued. In return, they offer unwavering support, advocacy, and forgiveness, making them a brand's most valuable asset.

The Non-Negotiable Rule: Brand Congruence

For a brand to build and maintain a strong fandom, it must obsess over consistency across all channels, touchpoints, and interactions. A brand cannot say one thing and do another. It cannot claim to stand for social responsibility while exploiting workers in its supply chain.

It cannot preach sustainability while engaging in environmentally harmful practices. If a brand walks like a duck and talks like a duck—it better be a duck.

The fatal flaw of many brands is that they either speak out of both sides of their mouth or fail to recognize that their actions matter more than their words. This inconsistency leads to mistrust and disengagement, eroding the emotional bond that fans have built.

In contrast, brands that maintain authenticity and alignment between their message and their actions develop an almost unbreakable connection with their audience. This is why companies like Patagonia, which champions sustainability, and Nike, which fuels self-empowerment through sport, have such dedicated followings. Their marketing isn't just about products—it's about purpose. And because their fans believe in why they exist, they remain fiercely loyal, even in challenging times.

From Brand to Movement

Fandom isn't built overnight, nor is it created through traditional transactional thinking. It is cultivated through emotional connection, brand integrity, and shared values—the principles that turn businesses into movements and consumers into lifelong believers.

The companies that understand this, embrace it, and execute it consistently will not just build brands; they will build icons that transcend commerce and become part of their fans' identities, aspirations, and daily lives.

And that is how you go from being just another brand to a legacy that lasts for generations--and shape culture.

Turning Strategy Into Action: How to Build Fandom Today

Understanding the psychology of fandom is crucial, but execution is everything. To move from theory to impact, brand leaders must actively foster trust, engagement, and emotional connection with their audience—fandom isn't built on products alone. To turn customers into lifelong fans, marketing leaders must shift from selling to cultivating relationships.

Here are five actionable steps to start building a devoted fandom today:

1. Align Brand Actions with Brand Values

Fandom thrives on authenticity. Consumers see through empty promises, and nothing kills brand loyalty faster than brand infidelity—when actions contradict values. If you stand for innovation, innovate. If you champion sustainability, embed it in everything you do.

- Actionable Step: Audit your brand's messaging and operations. Are you delivering on your values? Identify and fix misalignments immediately.

2. Move from Transactions to Relationships

Fans don't just buy; they belong. They crave engagement, recognition, and two-way interactions with the brands they love. If your audience feels unheard, they'll move on.

- Actionable Step: Engage daily—respond to comments, feature user-generated content, and co-create with your fans. Build participation, not just sales.

3. Build a Community, Not Just a Customer Base

Loyalty is tribal. Fans rally around shared experiences and identity, not just a product. Winning Brands like LEGO Ideas, Nike Running Clubs, and Harley-Davidson's H.O.G. create communities of fans, not markets.

- Actionable Step: Establish a fan ecosystem—host exclusive events, create VIP experiences, and build community-driven content. Make fans feel part of something bigger.

4. Leverage Storytelling to Deepen Emotional Connection

People don't buy what you sell—they buy why you exist. Storytelling is what transforms buyers into believers. Apple's "Think Different" campaign inspired. Red Bull fuels thrill-seekers. What's your story?

- Actionable Step: Craft a brand narrative that taps into emotion and identity—not just product features. If your story doesn't inspire, rewrite it.

5. Focus on Long-Term Loyalty Over Short-Term Gains

Discounts drive sales; fandom drives lifetime value. True fans stay loyal through price hikes, missteps, and competition—because they feel invested. Patagonia, Airbnb, and adidas don't compete on price, they compete on meaning.

- Actionable Step: Shift from acquisition to retention—reward loyalty with exclusive perks, premium access, and ongoing engagement. Keep fans emotionally connected beyond the purchase.

Final Thought: Fans Are Your Brand's Greatest Asset

Winning Brands aren't built by chance—they're built by design. Start implementing these five principles today, and begin your your journey to turn your brand into a cultural movement that lasts for generations.

From Customers to Fans: Identifying and Converting Your Audience

Your future fans are out there—but right now, they're just potential prospects, unaware of the emotional connection they could have with your brand. Just like a traditional customer funnel, there's a fan funnel, and it requires a completely different approach. Turning someone into a fan isn't about pushing a sale; it's about fostering a relationship.

To build a real fanbase, you need to move beyond the question of "what you can do for them" and focus on knowing who they are. What drives them? What values do they hold? What experiences shape their interests? The process isn't unlike dating—you don't just hand someone a list of features about yourself and expect them to fall in love. You have to understand what resonates with them on an emotional level and create meaningful interactions that build trust and loyalty.

Before you can attract fans, you must clearly define them. What are their demographics, interests, frustrations, and aspirations? How do they align with your brand's values, vision, and personality? Developing a consumer muse—a persona representing your ideal fan—will allow you to tailor your messaging and engagement strategies accordingly.

But first, let's make a critical distinction:

- Turning existing customers into fans (deepening loyalty and emotional investment).
- Unlocking new audiences who could transition into fans (expanding the reach and capturing new passionate advocates).

Both are essential, but they require two different strategies. A truly fan-driven brand maximizes both.

Finding Your Ideal Fans

Not all customers will become fans. Your job is to identify those most likely to form an emotional attachment to your brand—those who will advocate for you, engage with your content, and see your brand as part of their identity. This starts with analyzing consumer insights:

- Who already promotes your brand organically?
- Who is most active on social media, email campaigns, and live events?
- What shared values or behaviors unite your most passionate supporters?

A meaningful consumer insight requires seeing what everyone else has seen, but thinking what no one else has thought (Albert Szent-Gyorgyi).

Marketing has evolved from interruptions to genuine relationships.

In the 1970s, marketing was disruptive—TV commercials interrupted programming, and print ads interrupted articles. By the 1990s, brand activations and experiential marketing began shifting engagement from passive to participatory, offering consumers experiences rather than just advertisements. Today, with digital platforms and social media, marketing is fully immersive and interactive—an ongoing, two-way relationship between brands and their audiences.

This shift has fundamentally changed how consumers interact with content. Engagement is no longer one-directional—people are watching their favorite sports, movies, and events across multiple screens, hosting watch parties, co-streaming, creating memes, and participating in real-time discussions on Discord and Reddit. They are no longer just spectators—they are active participants in shaping brand culture.

To build real fandom, you need to step into your consumers' world. You won't find the most valuable insights by analyzing dashboards alone—you need real-world context. As the saying goes, If you want to understand how a tiger hunts, don't go to the zoo. Go to the jungle.

By immersing yourself in the lives of your audience, you gain a richer understanding of their emotional drivers, their daily experiences, and the pain points they face. This fan-first approach unlocks deeper storytelling, more relevant messaging, and stronger brand affinity—all critical components of turning casual customers into lifelong fans.

Beyond Demographics: Unlocking the Psychology of Brand Fans

Data provides information about consumer behavior, but true insights reveal the motivations behind it. These data can help you identify who are your most active, loyal, and satisfied fans.[9]

To identify your most passionate fans, start by analyzing how they engage with your brand online. Utilize tools like Google Analytics, Sprout Social for insights and brand sentiment, email marketing platforms, and customer relationship management (CRM) systems to track key engagement metrics—website visits, social media interactions (likes, comments, shares, mentions), reviews, ratings, email engagement (opens, clicks, replies), referrals, purchases, and loyalty indicators. These data points will help you pinpoint your most active, engaged, and loyal customers.

Beyond numbers, understanding the psychographics of your audience is crucial. Psychographics go deeper than basic demographics (age, gender, income) and focus on the values, interests, and lifestyle choices that drive purchasing decisions. What do your customers care about? What beliefs shape their behavior? Identifying these deeper motivations allows you to build a stronger emotional connection with your audience and convert casual buyers into lifelong fans.

Brands People Live By

Great brands don't just sell products; they sell identities, lifestyles, and values. The most successful companies go beyond demographics and tap into the deeper psychological motivators—beliefs, aspirations, and emotions—that drive consumer behavior. These brands cultivate loyalty by aligning with their audience's personal values and embedding themselves into their daily lives.

Here are four prime examples of brands that have mastered this approach:

---

[9] https://www.linkedin.com/advice/1/how-do-you-find-your-biggest-fans-skills-branding

Harley-Davidson: Freedom & Rebellion

Harley-Davidson's mission is simple yet powerful: *Freedom for the Soul.* It's not just about building motorcycles; it's about embracing the open road, independence, and a spirit of rebellion. Harley riders don't just buy a bike—they buy into a lifestyle that embodies adventure, self-expression, and an unbreakable sense of brotherhood. The brand's psychographic appeal is clear: it attracts individuals who value freedom, authenticity, and the thrill of the ride.

Nike: Empowerment & Achievement

Nike's mission—*To bring inspiration and innovation to every athlete* in the world* (**If you have a body, you are an athlete*)—is a masterclass in aspirational branding. Nike doesn't just sell athletic wear; it sells the drive to push boundaries, the will to compete, and the relentless pursuit of greatness. The *Just Do It* mantra reinforces a mindset of perseverance and overcoming obstacles, making Nike a beacon for those who see sports as a pathway to self-improvement.

Lululemon: Mindfulness & Community

Lululemon has built an empire around mindful wellness. More than a brand, it represents a way of life—one centered on health, yoga, and self-betterment. Beyond selling premium activewear, Lululemon fosters a sense of community through in-store experiences, local events, and ambassador programs. Its psychographic appeal is rooted in mindfulness, balance, and personal growth, attracting individuals who see wellness as a core part of their identity.

LEGO: Creativity & Future-Building

One of the most iconic brands in the world, LEGO[10] doesn't just make plastic bricks—it *inspires and develops the builders of tomorrow.* The brand's mission statement is an open invitation to creativity, innovation, and problem-solving. LEGO fans, from children to adult enthusiasts (AFOLs—Adult Fans of LEGO), aren't just buying toys; they are investing in

---

[10] https://www.lego.com/en-us/aboutus/lego-group/the-lego-brand

imagination, storytelling, and skill-building. The brand taps into the innate human desire to create, making it a lifelong passion for millions.

The LEGO® Brand Framework

Belief	Children are our role models
Mission	Inspire and develop the builders of tomorrow
Vision	A global force for Learning-through-Play
Idea	System-in-Play
Values	Imagination • Fun • Creativity • Caring • Learning • Quality
Promises	**Play** Promise — Play Well / **People** Promise — Succeed and Grow Together / **Planet** Promise — Positive Impact / **Partner** Promise — Mutual Value Creation
Spirit	Only the best is good enough

Each of these brands has successfully moved beyond the transactional model and into the emotional, identity-driven space where fandom thrives. They don't just market products; they connect with consumers on a deeper level, ensuring long-term loyalty and advocacy.

As a marketing leader, ask yourself: *What does my brand stand for beyond the product? What values and emotions am I tapping into?* Because when your brand aligns with the deeper aspirations of your audience, you're not just selling—you're creating something they can't imagine their lives without.

Understanding the deeper motivations of your fans goes beyond demographics and psychographics—it's also about knowing what they stand for. What causes do they support? What are they passionate about? By identifying the values that drive your audience, you can craft marketing strategies that truly resonate and build lasting loyalty.

The key is to develop a habit of constantly listening to your fans. Conduct surveys, host focus groups, and engage in meaningful conversations across social platforms. This ongoing process of gathering insights enables you to make data-driven decisions while ensuring your fans feel heard and valued.

Ask them directly: What do they love about your brand? What makes them feel connected? What do they expect from your products or services? Their answers will help refine your messaging, strengthen your positioning, and attract more people who align with your brand's essence.

And don't shy away from engaging with critics. Your most vocal detractors often provide the most unfiltered, valuable insights. Not to mention that these are the most vocal against your brand and company in social media, which can be an external threat to your growth. They highlight gaps, challenge assumptions, and force you to refine your brand's approach. Ignoring them won't make them go away—but addressing their concerns head-on can turn challenges into opportunities.

Keeping your friends close and your critics closer isn't just a defensive strategy—it's a proactive way to build a stronger, more resilient brand.

The Power of a Consumer Muse: The Key to a Fan-Centric Brand

It's interesting—ask a band, a musician, or a professional athlete about their fan base, and they can describe them in vivid detail. They know what their fans look like, what excites them, and what they care about. Now, ask a brand marketer the same question, and the response is often vague, incomplete, or purely demographic.

Why? Because musicians and athletes interact with their fans regularly. They perform for them, engage with them, and see firsthand what drives their enthusiasm. That's a lesson brands need to learn. How often do you see your customers? How often do you interact with them in a meaningful way? If you stay locked inside corporate offices, distanced from the people who matter most—your fans—you risk falling into the trap of status quo marketing.

Once you've identified your ideal fans, the next step is to build a detailed **consumer muse**—a living, evolving representation of your target audience, crafted from real data, insights, and behavioral patterns. Marketers are familiar with audience personas, but have you truly gotten inside your fans' heads? Understanding **what they buy** is one thing; understanding **why they buy** is where the real power lies.

Creating a consumer muse goes beyond demographics. It requires identifying the emotional triggers, values, and motivations that drive your fans. For example:

- A loyal millennial fan may prioritize sustainability, community engagement, and ethical consumerism.
- A tech-savvy Gen Z fan is likely drawn to innovation, digital-first experiences, and social connectivity.

These insights allow you to craft personalized, authentic messaging that makes fans feel seen and understood—not just sold to. The most successful brands do this seamlessly.

- Dove champions body positivity and inclusivity, building a loyal fan base around empowerment rather than just selling soap.
- Patagonia fosters environmental activism, encouraging customers to repair their clothing rather than replace it—aligning with their brand mission and deepening fan loyalty.

A well-defined consumer muse ensures consistency and congruence in every aspect of your branding—your messaging, campaigns, and interactions. It acts as your north star, guiding principles and keeping your brand aligned with the values that matter most to your audience. Knowing who you're speaking to and what they stand for transforms your brand from just another option in the market to a movement people actively want to be part of.

When a brand fully embraces its consumer muse, decision-making becomes more precise, storytelling becomes more authentic, and customer engagement deepens. But beyond just shaping marketing campaigns, a well-defined consumer muse serves as a strategic anchor— guiding product development, customer experiences, and even corporate values.

This level of clarity ensures that every touchpoint with the brand feels intentional and aligned with what truly matters to fans. It's not just about what a company wants to sell; it's about how it resonates with the people who matter most. When a brand consistently reflects the identity, values, and aspirations of its fans, it moves beyond transactions and into the realm of cultural significance.

And when that happens, brand affinity transforms into something far more powerful—**brand devotion**.

Understanding Fan Behavior:
What Drives Engagement and Loyalty?

So how do you turn customers into passionate, lifelong fans?

To build a true and lasting fandom, you need to understand the psychology of fan behavior—what they think, feel, and why they engage so deeply. What makes some people fiercely loyal to a brand for years, while others move on without hesitation? The answer lies in the emotional and psychological triggers that drive fandom.

Here are the core factors that fuel engagement and loyalty among brand fans:

- Emotional Connection – Fans connect with brands that evoke strong emotions—excitement, nostalgia, pride, or inspiration. This emotional bond makes them feel like they are part of something bigger than a mere transaction.

- Shared Values – Fans are drawn to brands that reflect their identity and beliefs. Whether it's sustainability, social justice, innovation, or self-expression, when a brand aligns with its values, they feel personally invested in its success.

- Brand Experience – Every interaction with a brand—whether through social media, customer service, or product use—shapes the overall experience. Delivering consistent, high-quality experiences ensures that customers transition from one-time buyers to devoted fans.

- Community – Fandom thrives on shared experiences. Brands that create spaces for fans to connect—whether through online forums, social media groups, or in-person events—cultivate a sense of belonging, strengthening the emotional bond between the fan and the brand.

Understanding these drivers allows you to design experiences that go beyond transactions and into deep emotional engagement. The goal is not just to sell a product but to create something that fans want to be a part of—something they are proud to champion. This is how brands move from being just another option in the market to becoming a cultural force.

What Makes Fans Stay Loyal?

Fandom isn't just about preference—it's about identity. When someone becomes a fan, they aren't just engaging with a brand; they are integrating it into their sense of self. This is why fandom is such a powerful driver of loyalty, advocacy, and emotional investment. But to fully harness its power, brands must understand the deeper psychological principles at play.

Here are some key insights into the psychology of fandom:

- Social Identity Theory – Fans see themselves as part of a collective, which provides a sense of belonging and validation. Supporting a brand or team isn't just about the product—it's about being part of a tribe that shares their values and interests.

- Emotional Attachment – The strongest fans develop deep emotional bonds with a brand, reacting to its successes and failures as if they were personal. Think about the frenzy surrounding an Apple product launch or the heartbreak of sports fans when their team loses—it's not just a brand to them; it's part of their identity.

- BIRGing (Basking in Reflected Glory) – Fans associate themselves with a brand's success, feeling a personal sense of accomplishment when it achieves something great. When Apple rebounded from near collapse in 1996 to become the world's most valuable company in 2010, its loyal customers didn't just watch—it felt like a victory they were part of.

- CORFing (Cutting Off Reflected Failure) – Just as fans celebrate victories, they may also distance themselves from a brand's failures to protect their self-esteem. If a brand missteps, fans may downplay their association or demand accountability to maintain the integrity of their emotional investment.

- "We" vs. "Them" Mentality – Fandom thrives on rivalry. Whether it's Apple vs. Android, Nike vs. adidas, or PlayStation vs. Xbox, fans define themselves not just by what they love, but also by what they oppose. This competitive dynamic strengthens loyalty and fuels engagement.

Understanding these dynamics is crucial because fandom is not passive—it is highly active and emotionally chargedl. Fans don't just buy from a brand; they defend it, advocate for it, and celebrate its wins as their own. But tapping into this psychology requires more than just selling a great product. It demands a deep understanding of what truly motivates your audience.

Building a strong, devoted fan base isn't something that happens by accident. It's a process that requires research, intentionality, and an ongoing commitment to fostering genuine relationships and personal connections. And while it's not easy, the brands that get it right don't just attract customers—they create movements.

Demographics vs. Psychographics: Going Beyond Basic Data

Think about your spouse, partner, or closest friend. How would you describe their personality? What kind of energy do they bring into a room? What motivates them? Now, apply the same level of curiosity to your brand's fans—both current and potential.

To truly understand brand fandom, you need to go beyond surface-level demographics. While demographic data—such as age, gender, income, and location—provides useful insights, it doesn't explain why people connect with your brand. Psychographics, on the other hand, uncover the deeper psychological factors that drive behavior. They help you answer essential questions:

- What do my fans truly care about?
- What drives their decision-making?
- What are their aspirations, struggles, and passions?

By identifying the emotional and psychological triggers behind consumer behavior, you gain powerful insights that enable you to forge stronger, more meaningful connections with your audience.

The Psychology of Fan Behavior: Disinhibition in Action

To better understand fandom, let's look at sports culture. Fans are known for their extreme emotional investment, but have you ever noticed how their behavior changes in certain settings? This is due to a social-psychological phenomenon known as **disinhibition**—a temporary loss of restraint in group settings, where emotions override normal social filters.

Think about what happens in a packed stadium. Even naturally reserved individuals will yell, chant, and high-five strangers when their team scores. The energy of the crowd fuels a sense of unity and shared experience, breaking down social barriers. This same effect can be seen in sports bars, where the collective excitement amplifies emotional reactions, sometimes to the point of chaos—especially after a major win or loss.

For brands, understanding this concept is crucial. When fans feel emotionally connected to a brand, they behave in similar ways—engaging in online discussions, creating user-generated content, defending the brand against criticism, and even making irrational purchasing decisions based purely on loyalty. Harnessing this level of engagement means creating spaces—both digital and physical—where fans can freely express their enthusiasm, reinforcing their emotional bond with your brand.

By tapping into both demographic and psychographic insights, you don't just identify your ideal fans—you learn how to turn their passion into participation.

So how can you get brand fans like that?!

If you want to create fans who live and breathe your brand—who engage, advocate, and even defend it—you need to understand what drives their passion and loyalty. Fans don't just buy from you; they believe in you. So, how do you build that kind of devotion?

Let's break it down with a **show-and-tell** approach.

1. Tap into the "In-Group vs. Out-Group" Phenomenon

Humans are wired for tribal loyalty—it's a fundamental part of our psychology. Sports teams have mastered this dynamic, creating fierce rivalries where fans identify as part of an exclusive in-group, setting themselves apart from an opposing out-group.

They are passionate about their teams, know every detail about the players, and religiously follow the progress of their hometown heroes. The only factor that differentiates these groups is the team they root for. Yet, people create arbitrary distinctions between the teams (and fans) they love and those they hate.[11]

Your brand can tap into this same tribal mentality by creating a distinct community identity. Consider:

- Apple vs. Android – Apple users don't just prefer iPhones; they see themselves as part of a culture of innovation, creativity, and exclusivity.

---

[11] https://www.psychologytoday.com/us/blog/fulfillment-any-age/201112/the-psychology-sports-fans

- Nike vs. adidas – Nike embodies a "Just Do It" ethos of relentless drive, while adidas leans into street culture and timeless style.

- Coca-Cola vs. Pepsi – Coke is the ambassador of tradition, and Pepsi is all about the next generation—a focus on youth demographics.

You don't have to create direct opposition to a competitor, but you **do** need to give fans a reason to feel part of something bigger than just a product. You're not just selling shoes, tech, or beverages—you're offering belonging.

- Action Step: Define what makes your brand's identity different. What do you stand for? What are you not? How do your fans see themselves in contrast to those who don't align with your brand?

2. Go Beyond Transactions—Create Shared Meaning

Demographics tell you who your customers are. Psychographics tell you why they care. If you want to build a fanbase, you must connect emotionally—not just sell.

Ask yourself:

- What does my brand stand for beyond the product?
- What values do my customers align with?
- How can my brand fit into their daily lives, passions, and identities?

Take Harley-Davidson—they don't just sell motorcycles; they sell the freedom of the open road. Their fans identify as rebels, adventurers, and non-conformists. That's why Harley owners tattoo the logo on their bodies—it's not just a brand, it's who they are.

- Action Step: Create messaging that speaks to your fans' identity, not just your product's features. Your brand should feel like an extension of who they are.

3. Foster Engagement and Community

Passionate fans don't exist in isolation—they thrive in communities. Whether it's online groups, events, or user-generated content, the most beloved brands make their fans feel like part of an inner circle.

Look at LEGO. Their LEGO Ideas platform allows fans to submit designs for potential new sets. The result? Fans become co-creators, deeply invested in the brand's success. It's no longer just a toy—it's a movement.

- Action Step: Find ways for fans to engage beyond purchasing. Can they contribute ideas? Get exclusive access? Be part of a challenge or event?

4. Make Your Fans the Heroes of Your Story

The best brands don't position themselves as the hero—they make their **fans the heroes**. Nike doesn't just sell shoes—they tell stories of athletes overcoming adversity. GoPro doesn't just sell cameras—they showcase the epic adventures of their users.

Your fans should feel seen, valued, and celebrated. When they do, they become evangelists, spreading your brand's message far and wide.

- Action Step: Highlight fan stories, user-generated content, or testimonials. Make them feel like they are the stars of the brand experience.

The Bottom Line

If you want fans who love your brand, you must create an identity, a movement, and a reason to belong. Fans don't form deep connections with companies that only see them as a transaction. They connect with brands that align with their values, passions, and identity.

By combining demographic insights (who they are) with psychographic insights (why they care), you don't just sell—you create a fandom. And that's how brands win hearts, not just wallets.

Bringing It Home: The Future of Fandom

Listening to your fans isn't just a marketing tactics—it's the foundation of brand longevity. The brands that thrive aren't the ones that shout the loudest; they're the ones that listen the closest. Your fans are constantly giving you the blueprint for success—through their excitement, their frustrations, their ideas, and their loyalty.

Ignore them, and they'll leave. Engage them, and they'll build your brand for you.

Fan feedback isn't just data—it's direction. It tells you what to double down on, what to refine, and where to take your brand next. The best part? Fans who feel heard don't just stick around—they recruit others.

So the real question is: Are you giving them something worth believing in?

Because in the next chapter, we're diving into what separates brands that fade from brands that become movements. Get ready. It's time to turn fandom into an unstoppable force.

CHAPTER 3
WHERE BRANDS
BECOME BELIEF.
THE POWER OF
FANDOM.

Every brand has customers, but not every brand has fans. And yet, the companies that thrive—the ones that transcend mere transactions and become cultural phenomena—are the ones that build true fandoms.

Fandom is more than loyalty; it's identity. It's what makes people camp outside Apple Stores for the latest iPhone, debate Marvel vs. DC with religious fervor, or wear their favorite sports team's jersey with unwavering pride.

But not all fans are the same. Just as customers vary in their engagement and buying habits, fandom exists on a spectrum. Some fans are die-hard evangelists, living and breathing your brand.

Others are casual supporters, engaging when it's convenient. Some are drawn in by influencers, while others rally around niche communities, subcultures, or shared nostalgia. Understanding these different types of fandom is essential for any brand leader who wants to harness the power of engaged, passionate supporters.

In this chapter, we'll break down the different types of fandom, how they behave, and—most importantly—how you can cultivate and nurture them. Whether your goal is to deepen loyalty, create a movement, or drive sustainable growth, knowing your fans on a deeper level is the key to unlocking the full potential of your brand.

Types of Fandom

Capturing Attention: The Power of Fandom

Just as no two customers are exactly alike, neither are your fans. Some engage with your brand daily, while others make occasional but significant purchases. Some are drawn in by a visionary founder, while others stay for the sense of belonging your brand fosters. The variety in consumer behavior isn't unique to your company—it's universal.

And the same principle applies to fandom.

Fandoms—communities of passionate, emotionally invested supporters—are one of the most powerful assets a brand can cultivate. But not all fans engage in the same way, and not all fandoms function alike. They have different motivations, different levels of commitment, and different ways of amplifying your brand. Understanding these distinctions is essential to fostering meaningful connections and maximizing brand advocacy.

Consider the cultural impact of some of the world's most passionate fandoms:

- Potterheads (Harry Potter Fans)
- Swifties (Taylor Swift fans)
- Marvel Enthusiasts (MCU Fans)
- Manchester United Supporters (Football fans with global reach)
- Clemson Tigers Alumni (College Football fanatics)

In the business world, **some brands have sustained legendary fandoms** for decades—Nike, Apple, LEGO, Disney, and Mercedes, to name a few. Meanwhile, newer brands like Starbucks, YouTube, Spotify, and Instagram have quickly built their own legions of dedicated followers. The common thread? These brands create identity, culture, and build communities.

Hyperfocus

The Need For Hyperfocus

The brands that had the most success this year were the ones that weren't afraid to double down on niches.

Brands like Nike, Gymshark, Guinness and Bose were all applauded by fans for their dedication to impacting fan groups that have disproportionate influence on sport and gaming communities.

Number 1 brand Nike had 5x more unprompted mentions from fans than adidas, showing that the biggest brand in sport and lifestyle still dominates the conversation.

The reason for success? A hyperfocused approach they take to the masses, supercharging their ability to win with young, influential audiences.

These brands haven't abandoned reaching mass audiences. Instead, they've combined huge reach with a focused commitment to highly influential fans to create cultural impact.

Hard court specialist.

Fan Intelligence® Index 24/25   19

And with the rise of digital culture, fandom has evolved. The riches are in the niches, and the most successful brands understand how to cultivate, engage, and activate these communities.

In this chapter, we'll break down the different types of fandoms, how they form, how they behave, and—most importantly—how your brand can harness their power. Ready? Let's dive in.

The Enthusiast Fandom:
Passionate Advocates Who Live and Breathe Your Brand

The **Enthusiast Fandom** represents the most dedicated and fervent supporters of your brand—your die-hard fans. These are the people who camp outside Apple Stores days before a product launch, or Swifties who wait in line for a week just to be front row at a concert. They don't just love your brand—they live it.

But their value extends far beyond their personal loyalty. Enthusiasts are not only repeat customers; they are **brand evangelists** who actively promote your products, engage with your content, and help shape the perception of your brand in the marketplace. They don't just buy—they advocate.

Characteristics of Enthusiast Fans

- Unmatched Passion – Enthusiasts are emotionally invested in your brand. Their excitement borders on obsession, and they take pride in spreading the word. They don't just use your product; they integrate it into their identity and lifestyle.

- Evangelism and Advocacy – These fans are your most vocal champions. They influence others through organic word-of-mouth, whether by posting reviews, sharing brand experiences, or persuading friends and family to switch to your brand.

- High Engagement – Enthusiasts are hyperactive participants in your brand's ecosystem. They attend your events, engage with your brand on social media, and provide direct feedback. They fuel conversations in online communities, forums, and fan groups, keeping your brand relevant and top of mind.

How to Nurture Enthusiast Fandom

- Create Exclusive Content – Offer behind-the-scenes access, early product releases, and exclusive content that makes them feel like insiders. These fans crave deeper connections with the brand.

- Foster a Sense of Belonging – Enthusiasts want to be part of something bigger. Build an exclusive membership program or a community that recognizes their loyalty and integrates them into the brand's story.

- Encourage User-Generated Content – Give fans a platform to showcase their passion. Whether through social media challenges, fan art, or video testimonials, amplifying their voices strengthens their connection to the brand and encourages further engagement.

Why Do They Matter?

Enthusiast fans are the lifeblood of brand fandom. Their passion creates momentum, attracting more fans and shaping a powerful brand narrative. Unlike traditional marketing, their advocacy is genuine and unpaid—making it far more influential. Their ability to generate organic buzz, defend the brand against criticism, and act as trusted sources of recommendations makes them an indispensable asset.

Simply put, the more Enthusiast Fans you cultivate, the stronger and more resilient your brand becomes.

The Casual Fandom:
Building Brand Affinity Without Full Commitment

While Enthusiast Fans are fully immersed in your brand, Casual Fans maintain a more passive yet positive relationship with it. They enjoy your products, make occasional purchases, and hold a favorable opinion of your brand—but they don't engage at the same level of intensity. These individuals are brand-aware and brand-friendly, but their loyalty is often dictated by convenience, price, or competitive alternatives.

However, here's where the real opportunity lies: Casual fans can evolve into passionate brand advocates. The key is understanding how to nurture, engage, and gradually move them up the loyalty ladder—from occasional buyers to lifelong fans.

Characteristics of Casual Fans

- Occasional Purchasers – They buy from your brand sporadically but don't exhibit the habitual purchasing behavior of an enthusiast.

- Brand Affinity – They have a generally positive perception of your brand but lack the deep emotional investment that drives advocacy and loyalty.

- Lower Engagement – Casual fans may follow your brand on social media or occasionally read an email, but they are far less likely to actively participate, share content, or engage in meaningful conversations.

How to Convert Casual Fans Into Enthusiasts

- Loyalty Programs That Reward Engagement – Offer structured incentives for repeat purchases, referrals, and ongoing engagement. Programs that provide exclusive perks, priority access, and limited-edition products can reinforce a sense of value and belonging.

- Gamification of Engagement – Turn participation into an experience. Habit-forming behaviors can be encouraged by rewarding fans with status recognition, unlocking achievements, and creating tiered loyalty levels that elevate the most engaged users.

- Strategic Content That Adds Value – Provide engaging, relevant content that resonates with casual fans—whether it's educational resources, behind-the-scenes insights, or interactive storytelling. The goal is to increase their emotional connection to the brand and position it as more than just a transactional choice.

- Create a Sense of Exclusivity – People want to be part of something special. Introduce member-only events, VIP experiences, and first-look previews to spark curiosity and deepen engagement. Casual fans who feel valued are far more likely to transition into loyal brand advocates.

Why Do Casual Fans Matter?

Casual fans make up a significant portion of your audience. While they may not seem as valuable as your die-hard supporters, they represent a massive growth opportunity. By strategically nurturing and converting them into more engaged participants, you build a sustainable, scalable fandom.

If your brand currently has a broad base of casual fans, this is where your biggest potential lies. With intentional commitment and a fan-first mindset, you can transform occasional buyers into enthusiastic evangelists—the kind of supporters who don't just consume your brand but champion it.

The Niche Fandom:
Connecting with Specialized Audiences

Before diving into niche fandoms, let's first define what a niche market is. A niche market is a segment of a larger market that is distinguished by unique needs, preferences, or identity. For example, vegan face wash is a niche within the broader face wash market. No matter the industry, there are always submarkets that cater to specific customer demands.

Common ways to define a niche market include[12]:

- Price – Luxury vs. budget-conscious consumers
- Demographics – Age, gender, occupation, or lifestyle-based segmentation
- Quality Level – Premium craftsmanship vs. mass-market appeal
- Geographic Area – Hyperlocal markets or region-specific products

Some brands thrive entirely within niche markets, cultivating a loyal and engaged following. Consider Untuckit, a brand built around a single, highly specific need—button-down shirts designed to be worn untucked. While a small subset of the larger fashion industry, this focus has created a dedicated fanbase. Another example is Drybar, a brand specializing exclusively in blowout hairstyling for women. By catering to a specific and passionate audience, they've cultivated deep brand loyalty.

---

[12] https://mirasee.com/blog/niche-market-examples/

The Internet and the Rise of Niche Fandoms

We live in an increasingly segmented world, where consumers seek out brands that cater to their specific needs and interests. The ability to build niche fan communities has exploded over the past two decades—thanks to the Internet.

Try building a niche fandom in 1985—it was significantly harder. Without digital tools, businesses relied on traditional advertising, word of mouth, and brick-and-mortar retail to reach their audience. Finding and nurturing specialized audiences was an uphill battle. Today, however, social media, digital communities, and targeted marketing make it easier than ever to connect with, engage, and grow niche fandoms.

The Power of Niche Fandoms

Niche fandoms may be smaller in size, but they are often highly engaged, deeply loyal, and more emotionally connected than broader audiences. These fans aren't just casually interested—they are invested in your brand because it speaks directly to their unique identity, needs, or passions.

Unlike mass-market audiences, niche fans actively seek out brands that cater to them. They may not engage with your brand as a whole, but if you serve their specific needs exceptionally well, they will support you passionately, advocate for you, and stick with you long-term.

For brands that understand how to cultivate niche fandoms, the opportunities are endless. Instead of trying to appeal to everyone, focus on deeply resonating with the right audience— because in today's world, the riches are in the niches.

EAR TO THE GROUND   Hyperfocus

Three

Find Your Niche

ANALYSIS

`FAN_INTELLIGENCE_AI`

The Past:
Brands were appreciated for providing platforms that allowed athletes and gamers to shine in front of the biggest audience possible.

The Future:
Fans value brands that are deeply focused on specific communities, where support is a sign of genuine commitment.

Attracts:

Decide whose cup of tea you actually want to be, then go all in.

Audiences love brands that get specific about their audience - like Gymshark speaking to true gym-heads in a language they understand.

"Gymshark focuses on not only building a physically stronger community, but a mentally stronger one too. They know what values matter to the community because they are in the community themselves"

Repels:

There's a constant temptation to be all things to all people, but this is a recipe for mediocrity.

Axe fell in the rankings this year - a brand with strong heritage in both sport and gaming - because they haven't consistently shown up.

'I gave Axe a low score because they haven't changed their narrative. It feels like they position themselves in sports because it's popular, but there's no real connection. It's like, 'Oh, we're a brand for athletes,' but they haven't done the work to really integrate into the community'.

CHICKEN, RICE, & BROCCOLI FOR DINNER. AGAIN.

GYMSHARK WE DO GYM

Characteristics of Niche Fans: Why They Matter

Niche fandoms may be smaller in size, but their impact is disproportionately powerful. Unlike broad audiences that engage with brands on a superficial level, niche fans are deeply invested—they are loyal, passionate, and highly engaged advocates. These individuals don't just purchase products; they see the brand as an extension of their identity.

Key Traits of Niche Fans

- Highly Specialized Interests: These fans are drawn to brands that cater to specific needs, subcultures, or lifestyles. Whether it's high-performance cycling gear, a rare collectible sneaker line, or a particular diet like vegan or keto, their interests are deeply defined.

- Tight-Knit Communities: Niche fandoms thrive within small, highly engaged communities where fans connect, share insights, and reinforce their loyalty to the brand. These groups form online (forums, social media, Discord servers) or in-person through specialized events and meetups.

- Exclusive Loyalty: While niche audiences may not represent the largest customer segment, they often exhibit unparalleled commitment to the brands they love. Because the brand speaks directly to their unique passions, they develop a sense of belonging— making them highly resistant to switching to competitors.

How to Build and Engage Niche Fandoms

To successfully cultivate a niche fandom, brands must go beyond traditional marketing tactics and actively engage with their audience in meaningful ways.

- Targeted Messaging: Speak directly to your niche audience's specific needs, values, and aspirations. Generic marketing doesn't work here—authenticity and relevance are key.

- Foster Community: Create dedicated spaces for your fans to connect. This can include private online groups, exclusive content, brand-hosted events, or interactive experiences where fans can engage with one another and strengthen their connection to the brand.

- Be Authentic: Niche fans are highly discerning—they can instantly recognize when a brand is faking interest in their community. Ensure your brand truly aligns with the interests, beliefs, and culture of the niche. Authenticity builds trust, and trust builds lifelong fandom.

Why Do Niche Fandoms Matter? The Business Impact

The power of niche fandoms extends far beyond their smaller audience size—they deliver exceptional levels of loyalty, advocacy, and long-term revenue growth.

Loyal Fans Have a Higher Lifetime Value (LTV):

A loyal fan generates 2-10 times more revenue over their lifetime compared to a casual customer, depending on the industry and business model. This is due to:

- Higher purchase frequency – They return to buy from the brand again and again.

- Higher average order value – They invest more in premium products or services.

- Longer customer lifespan – Their emotional attachment extends the duration of their relationship with the brand[13].

Word-of-Mouth and Brand Trust Drive Sales:

Trust has become an essential factor in purchasing decisions. According to research[14]:

- 71% of consumers say that trusting a brand is more important today than ever before.

- This sentiment is even stronger among Gen Z consumers (ages 18-26), with 79% emphasizing the importance of brand trust.

- Despite valuing trust more than any other generation, Gen Z is also the most skeptical of brands, making authentic engagement with niche fandoms a critical success factor.

---

[13] https://strivecloud.io/blog/cltv-improves-loyalty/#:~:text=Start%20with%20determining%20the%20average,adds%20up%20to%20%E2%82%AC12%2C000.

[14] https://www.marketingcharts.com/brand-related/brand-metrics-230034#:~:text=The%20analysts%20suggest%20that%20these,advocate%20for%20such%20a%20brand.

Consumers' Heightened Need to Trust Brands

"It is more important to trust the brands I buy or use today than in the past"

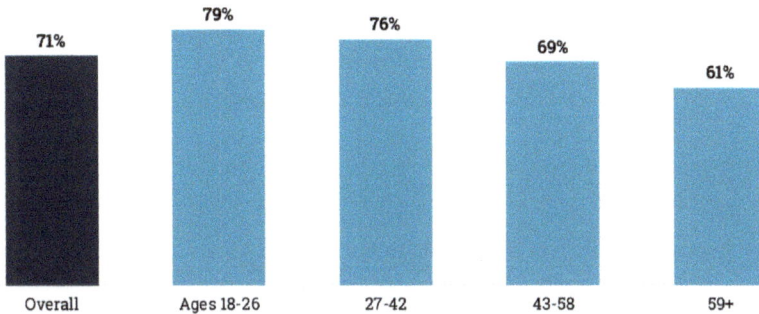

marketing charts

	Overall	Ages 18-26	27-42	43-58	59+
	71%	79%	76%	69%	61%

Published on MarketingCharts.com in June 2023 | Data Source: Edelman
Based on a May survey of 13,802 adults across 14 countries:
Brazil; Canada; China; France; Germany; India; Japan; Mexico; Saudi Arabia; South Africa; South Korea; UAE; UK; and US.

The Bottom Line: Niche Fans Are Your Brand's Secret Weapon

Niche fandoms may not have the scale of mass-market audiences, but their influence is profound. They spend more, stay longer, and become vocal brand advocates who fuel organic growth through word-of-mouth marketing and community-driven engagement.

Brands that understand how to cultivate niche fandoms don't just sell products—they become part of their fans' identities. And when that happens, your brand isn't just another option in the marketplace—it becomes irreplaceable.

The Influencer Fandom:
Leveraging Creators to Amplify Your Brand

In the age of social media, influencers—also known as "Content Creators"—hold tremendous power in shaping audience perceptions and behaviors. The Influencer Fandom is built around key opinion leaders who act as brand amplifiers, extending your reach and reinforcing credibility through authentic connections with your followers.

Unlike traditional brand loyalty, these fans are primarily followers of the influencer first. However, their admiration and trust in the creator often spill over to the brands they endorse. When done right, influencer marketing doesn't just promote products—it builds a fan-driven ecosystem where brands become an integral part of an influencer's content, identity, and community.

Influencers as Brand Catalysts: A Real-World Example

One of the most successful brands leveraging influencer marketing is Lynda.com, a leading online learning platform (now part of LinkedIn Learning). Rather than relying on traditional ads, Lynda partnered with top YouTube influencers such as Rooster Teeth and The Fine Brothers—trusted content creators with millions of engaged followers.

Through strategic placements, influencer Jack Douglass seamlessly incorporated Lynda's offerings into his regular video content, making it feel organic rather than promotional. As a result, this campaign reached over 46 million YouTube subscribers, with many of the videos generating over one million views each[15].

This case study underscores a key principle: when influencers integrate a brand into their content authentically, their fans don't just see an ad—they experience a recommendation from someone they trust.

Characteristics of Influencer/Creator Fans

- Social Media-Centric Engagement – These fans primarily interact with brands via social media, actively following, liking, commenting, and sharing influencer-generated content.

- Trust and Credibility – Influencers humanize brands, making their endorsements feel genuine rather than transactional. This trust significantly impacts purchasing behavior, as consumers are more likely to try a brand recommended by someone they admire.

- Broad and Fragmented Reach – Unlike niche fandoms, influencer fans span across multiple demographics and interests. While this reach is valuable, it also means fandom loyalty may be more attached to the influencer than the brand itself.

How to Effectively Leverage Influencer Fandom

- Choose the Right Influencers: Partner with creators whose values and audience align with your brand, ensuring a natural fit. Forced or inauthentic collaborations can backfire, eroding trust.

- Encourage Authentic Storytelling: Give influencers creative freedom to integrate your brand into their content naturally, rather than forcing a scripted ad. The best influencer partnerships feel seamless and engaging rather than disruptive.

---

[15] https://grin.co/blog/brands-using-influencer-marketing/

- Foster Long-Term Relationships: A one-off sponsored post won't build lasting brand loyalty. Ongoing collaborations help solidify the connection between the influencer, their audience, and your brand—turning casual followers into true brand fans.

Why Influencer Fandoms Matter

Influencer fandoms represent one of the most powerful marketing tools in today's digital landscape. By leveraging trusted voices, brands can break through the noise and reach audiences in an authentic, engaging way.

However, brands must recognize that influencer-driven fandoms are often tied more to the creator than the product itself. This means companies must nurture these fans beyond the initial introduction, ensuring that the brand itself—not just the influencer—becomes a source of value and connection.

When executed strategically, influencer marketing isn't just about endorsements—it's about embedding your brand into digital culture, shaping conversations, and converting casual viewers into devoted brand advocates.

The Fanatic Fandom:
Harnessing Extreme Loyalty for Brand Advocacy

Fanatic fans represent the pinnacle of brand devotion. These individuals aren't just loyal customers—they are fierce advocates, vocal defenders, and active promoters of your brand. Their emotional investment transcends the transactional relationship, making them one of the most valuable assets a company can cultivate.

These fans don't just buy your products—they live and breathe your brand. They rally behind your mission, defend your reputation, and spread your message with unwavering passion. Their enthusiasm is contagious, influencing others to engage, purchase, and commit to the brand on a deeper level.

Want to know what a fanatic fandom looks like? Here are some prime examples of brands with unmatched levels of devotion:

- Google – So ubiquitous that its name is now a verb in the Merriam-Webster dictionary.

- Linux – An open-source brand that built a devoted programming community, symbolized by its iconic Tux the Penguin.

- Disney – Encourages fan participation through activities like Disney bounding, fan art, and immersive storytelling.

- TikTok – Cultivated a grassroots fandom by fostering sub-communities and celebrating original creators.

- Apple – Ranked #1 for customer loyalty in the U.S. in 2023, with fans who defend and promote the brand fiercely.

- Angel City Football Club – A sports brand that has built an emotional connection with its fans through purpose-driven engagement.

Characteristics of Fanatic Fans

- Vocal Advocacy: Fanatics don't just love your brand—they actively defend, promote, and evangelize it. They advocate for your brand as if it were a cause, not just a company.

- Emotional Attachment: Their connection to your brand runs deeper than the product—they identify with your mission, values, and purpose. Your brand is an extension of who they are.

- Extreme Loyalty: These are the fans who will camp out for product launches, travel long distances for events, and go out of their way to engage with your brand—no matter the cost or inconvenience.

How to Nurture and Empower Fanatic Fans

- **Make the Brand Their Platform**

Give fanatics the opportunity to lead, create, and represent your brand. Feature them in campaigns, user-generated content, and community-driven events. The more ownership they feel, the stronger their advocacy will be.

- **Provide Exclusive Perks & 'Money-Can't-Buy' Experiences**

Offer VIP access, behind-the-scenes content, or first access to new products, events, and innovations. Fanatic fans crave exclusivity—give them something that reinforces their elite connection with your brand.

- **Recognize & Celebrate Their Loyalty**

Publicly acknowledge and celebrate fanatic fans—feature their stories, showcase their content, or create special rewards for their unwavering advocacy. A simple act of appreciation can strengthen their commitment even further.

Why Fanatic Fans Matter

- They are your ultimate brand evangelists. Their influence extends beyond personal consumption—they actively recruit new fans, defend your brand, and shape public perception.

- They amplify your brand without paid marketing. Their word-of-mouth advocacy is more powerful than any advertisement, providing authentic credibility that money can't buy.

- They create cultural relevance. Winning Brands don't just sell products; they create movements. Fanatic fans turn brands into lifestyle choices, social status symbols, and communities.

Final Thought: Fanatic Fans Are Your Brand's Superpower

The brands that truly understand, empower, and celebrate their most devoted fans will cultivate not just customers, but movements. These fans don't just represent brand loyalty—they are the fuel that turns a great brand into an icon. So, the question is—are you nurturing the fans who will take your brand to the next level?

Subculture Fandoms:
Tapping Into Movements and Countercultures

Ah, subcultures—a word that sounds a little rebellious, maybe even a bit underground. And that's the point. Some might call them "cult" fandoms (which, let's be honest, doesn't exactly scream mass appeal). But here's the truth: subcultures drive culture forward. What starts as niche, underground, or countercultural often becomes mainstream.

Look at Patagonia—once a brand for hardcore climbers and environmental activists, now a household name for anyone who *wants* to look like they care about the planet. Ben & Jerry's? Started as a hippie ice cream brand, and now it's in nearly every grocery store freezer. The animé fandom was once a niche community of die-hard fans trading VHS tapes—now it's a billion-dollar industry with global appeal.

Subcultures aren't just fringe groups; they are the breeding ground for trends that redefine industries. If you want to build a brand with lasting impact, pay attention to subcultures—because they're where real movements begin.

Understanding Subculture Fandom

At the heart of subculture fandom lies passion, identity, and authenticity. These fans aren't just casual consumers—they are deeply engaged participants who live and breathe the values of the subculture. They aren't just buying a product; they are investing in a lifestyle, a belief system, a movement.

Take streetwear culture, for example. Brands like Supreme and adidas don't just sell clothing—they sell an identity rooted in creativity, rebellion, and self-expression. The same applies to brands tied to social causes, activism, or countercultural movements.

Patagonia isn't just about outdoor gear—it's a symbol of environmental activism. Fans don't just wear the brand; they align with its mission. That's why Patagonia's fanbase isn't just loyal—it's evangelical.

Want your brand to tap into subcultures that create lifelong fans? You can't fake it. Here's how to do it right.

EAR TO THE GROUND   Hyperfocus

Passion Points

Choose them carefully.

Fans are not one-size-fits-all. If you think the same rules apply across all passion points, you're mistaken.

Nowhere is this contrast more evident than between sports and gaming fans.

Some brands resonate with both groups, others connect with just one, and many struggle to reach either.

To succeed, brands need a focused, tailored approach that recognises the unique needs of sports and gaming fans.

Fan Intelligence® Index 24/25   27

Strategies for Engaging Subculture Fans

Authenticity or Nothing

Subculture fans sniff out corporate pandering like sharks smell blood. If you're trying to cash in without truly understanding the culture, they will reject you—loudly. Instead of forcing your way in, immerse yourself in the subculture. Listen before you speak. Participate before you sell.

Collaborate with Key Opinion Leaders (KOLs)

Want credibility? Partner with people **who already have it**.

- adidas didn't just enter the streetwear and hip-hop scene—they partnered with Beyonce, Stella McCartney and Pharell Williams, solidifying their cultural relevance.
- Red Bull didn't just advertise extreme sports—they built an entire culture around it, sponsoring events and collaborating with top athletes.
- Nike tapped into sneaker culture by dropping limited-edition collaborations that feel more like collector's items than just another product release.

Tell Stories That Resonate

You can't market to subcultures from the outside. You need insider knowledge. Your brand needs to tell stories that feel like they were written by the community, for the community.

- Vans didn't just slap a logo on shoes—they embedded themselves in skate culture, sponsoring events, supporting artists, and staying true to their rebellious DNA.
- Patagonia's marketing isn't about selling jackets—it's about saving the planet. That's why their fans buy-in, not just buy.

Another Great Example: Vans – The Ultimate Subculture Brand

Vans has mastered the art of subculture fandom. It started in the skateboarding world, where it was adopted as the unofficial shoe of rebellion. But unlike many brands that lose credibility when they go mainstream, Vans has managed to stay true to its roots while expanding its audience.

How? By never abandoning the subculture that built it.

- They sponsor skate events, music festivals, and street art movements.

- They collaborate with underground artists and counterculture icons.

- They don't just sell shoes—they sell an identity.

The pattern is clear: Subcultures create icons. Brands that tap into them the right way become movements, not just businesses.

Final Thought: Don't Chase Culture—Earn Your Place In It

Brands that understand the power of subcultures don't just attract customers—they build tribes. They create meaning, not just marketing. They don't force their way into culture—they become part of it.

So, the question isn't whether subcultures matter. The question is: Is your brand worthy of being part of one?

The Nostalgic Fandom:
Reviving Past Connections with Legacy Fans

Vinyl records, anyone? Once thought to be obsolete, vinyl is now more popular than it was in 1970—despite being nearly extinct by 1995. Nostalgia isn't just a passing trend; it's an emotional powerhouse that can reignite old connections, strengthen brand loyalty, and even drive new customer engagement.

Legacy fans—those who have had a long-standing relationship with a brand—are a goldmine of opportunity. They've already experienced the brand's journey and, if engaged properly, can be reinvigorated into passionate advocates once again.

The Power of Nostalgia

For many consumers, a brand isn't just a product—it's part of their personal history. The toys they played with as kids, the car their parents drove, the cereal they ate on Saturday mornings—these brands are deeply woven into their memories. Tapping into those emotional connections can bring back dormant fans and create new ones.

But nostalgia isn't just for older generations. Younger consumers—millennials and Gen Z—are actively embracing retro culture. Why? Because nostalgia provides an authentic analog experience and an opportunity to disconnect from a world of constant digital stimulation. That's why vinyl records, Polaroid cameras, and even flip phones are making a comeback.

Case in point: The Vinyl Revival.

Streaming platforms like Spotify, Apple Music, and Tidal have made access to music easier than ever—but something got lost along the way: ownership. Vinyl brings back the ritual of music consumption. Selecting a record, placing it on a turntable, and physically engaging with an album create a deeper, more personal experience. The resurgence of vinyl isn't just about better sound quality—it's about human connection to a tangible and personal experience[16].

For brands, the lesson is clear: Consumers crave meaningful connections to the past—brands that successfully tap into nostalgia can unlock an entirely new level of fandom.

Strategies for Engaging Nostalgic Fans

Reintroduce Classic Products

Reviving iconic products can spark excitement among legacy fans while introducing a new generation to your brand.

- *Example: Nintendo's relaunch of retro gaming consoles brought nostalgic joy to older gamers while capturing younger audiences curious about classic gaming.*

Leverage Storytelling

Use visuals, messaging, and campaigns that evoke **strong memories** and reinforce your brand's legacy.

- *Example: Coca-Cola regularly integrates vintage ads and holiday campaigns, reminding consumers of its deep-rooted presence in their lives.*

Modernize Legacy: Blend nostalgia with innovation. Legacy brands can refresh classic products while maintaining the emotional essence that made them iconic.

- *Example: The Ford Bronco returned with modern upgrades while staying true to its rugged, adventurous spirit.*

---

[16] https://www.stozzaudio.com/home/why-vinyl-is-making-a-comeback-in-the-digital-age

Amplify Through Influencers & Testimonials: Engage long-time customers to share their experiences, emphasizing multi-generational relationships with the brand.

- *Example: Levi's celebrates denim culture by featuring customers who've worn their jeans for decades—solidifying its place as a timeless brand.*

Reignite, Reimagine, Repeat: The Disney Fandom Formula

If there's one brand that understands nostalgia, it's Disney.

Disney's live-action remakes of animated classics are prime examples of blending nostalgia with contemporary storytelling. By introducing beloved films like *The Lion King, Aladdin, and Beauty and the Beast* with new technology, Disney reconnects older audiences with their childhood while introducing younger generations to timeless stories.

And it doesn't stop there—Disney has cultivated multiple fandoms across different generations, from classic *Mickey Mouse* lovers to *Star Wars* and *Marvel* enthusiasts.

For brands looking to reignite legacy fans and attract new ones, Disney's strategy proves that nostalgia isn't about looking back—it's about bringing the past forward in a way that feels fresh, relevant, and deeply personal.

Nostalgia Isn't a Trend—It's a Growth Strategy

Nostalgia isn't just about sentimental value—it's a powerful marketing tool that drives loyalty, engagement, and revenue. The brands that understand how to re-engage legacy fans while appealing to new audiences will continue to win in the long run.

So ask yourself: What's the most nostalgic aspect of your brand? And how can you use it to spark an emotional connection today?

The Community Fandom:
The Power of Connection and Belonging

Community fandom is one of the most powerful and relevant strategies for brands today. Why? Because it transforms customers into a self-sustaining network of loyal advocates—people who don't just engage with the brand but also with one another. When fans feel like they belong, brand loyalty moves beyond transactions and into identity.

The unlock? Integrate your brand into the heart of the community you want to build emotional connections with. When your brand becomes a shared experience, rather than just a product or service, fans don't just support it—they live it.

Why Community Fandom Matters

Humans are wired for connection. Fans don't just want to consume content or buy products; they want to belong to something bigger than themselves. They seek spaces where they can share their passions, experiences, and excitement with like-minded individuals.

Brands that facilitate these connections don't just create customers—they create movements.

Whether it's a Discord server, a Reddit forum, a local meetup, or an interactive brand platform, creating these spaces deepens emotional investment and turns passive supporters into active community builders. And the best part? The more connected fans become to each other, the stronger their connection to the brand.

Community fandom isn't just about engagement—it's about creating a cultural gravitational pull that keeps fans invested.

Strategies for Building Fan Communities

Create Online Platforms: Develop digital spaces where fans can interact, share, and engage with your brand and each other.

- *Example: Nike's Run Club app allows runners to track progress, celebrate achievements, and connect with a global community of like-minded athletes.*

Host Offline Events: In-person experiences build a deeper sense of belonging and create memories that forge emotional ties.

- *Example: Red Bull's extreme sports events bring their community together, reinforcing the brand's identity beyond just energy drinks.*

Encourage User-Generated Content: Encourage your fans to recreate your brand's story in their own words. When you invite participation—through social media challenges, user-generated content (UGC), or fan-created content—you build a sense of ownership. This not only deepens engagement but also brings authenticity that can't be manufactured.

- *Example: GoPro built its community around user-generated adventure videos, making fans the face of the brand.*

Recognize and Reward Fans: Make your most engaged community members feel valued by acknowledging their contributions and offering **exclusive experiences, early access, or elevated status within the community**.

- *Example: Sephora's Beauty Insider program not only rewards purchases but also fosters engagement with an exclusive online community.*

The Rebirth of LEGO: A Case Study in Community Fandom

Few brands have mastered community fandom as brilliantly as LEGO.

Once struggling to stay relevant, LEGO revived its brand by listening to its community and giving fans a role in shaping its future. The LEGO Ideas platform allows fans to submit their own designs for potential new sets, with the most popular designs getting produced as official LEGO products.

What's the result?

- Fans feel like co-creators, strengthening their connection to the brand.
- LEGO isn't just selling toys; it's empowering imagination and participation.
- The brand benefits from crowdsourced innovation, reducing product development risk.

LEGO's resurgence proves that community isn't just a marketing strategy—it's a growth engine. When a brand fosters a shared sense of ownership, belonging, and creative participation, it doesn't just build fandom—it builds a legacy.

Final Thought: The Future of Fandom is Community-Driven

If your brand isn't building a community, you're missing the most powerful fandom strategy available.

Forget the outdated approach of shouting your message at customers. Today, the strongest brands build spaces where fans drive the conversation themselves.

So, ask yourself:

- How can you create shared experiences that connect fans not just to your brand, but to each other?

- What spaces can you build—online or offline—where fans feel seen, valued, and engaged?

- How can you turn customers into community leaders who carry your brand forward?

The brands that unlock community fandom aren't just selling products—they're creating movements.

The Event-Driven Fandom:
The Rise of Super Events & IRL Experiences

Live. In person. Full immersion.

Welcome to the era of super events, where fans aren't just watching from the sidelines—they're stepping into the brand experience. Whether it's a sold-out concert, a product launch, a pop-up activation, or a global convention, fans are craving real-life interactions that go beyond digital engagement.

This is the next evolution of fandom—where brands create not just a following, but an entire world that fans can step into, feel, and belong to.

Why Events Matter More Than Ever

Experiences are everything. We're living in a time when consumers prioritize experiences over possessions. People aren't just buying products anymore—they're investing in moments, memories, and identity.

- Experiences create deep emotional bonds—you never forget an incredible memory.

- Live events forge a sense of belonging—people want to feel part of a movement.

- IRL experiences drive organic marketing—fans share, post, and spread the word.

Just look at Disney's theme park superfans. Some people visit Disneyland or Disney World 50 or 100 times in their lifetime—because it's not just about the rides; it's about being part of a world that feels like home.

How to Build Fandom Through Events

The best brands don't just host events—they create IRL brand ecosystems. Here's how:

Host Exclusive Gatherings: Give fans something **they can't get anywhere else**—VIP experiences, early access, or behind-the-scenes looks.

- *Example: Sneaker brands like Jordan hold limited-access launch events, turning every release into a cultural moment.*

Participate in Industry Conventions: Go where the **most passionate fans already gather**—tech expos, gaming conventions, fashion weeks, and more.

- *Example: Comic-Con isn't just for movies—it's where brands engage with die-hard fans of storytelling, creativity, and collectibles.*

Create Immersive Pop-Ups: Temporary experiences with high impact. Think interactive brand playgrounds, Instagram-worthy moments, and hands-on demos.

- *Example: Glossier's pop-up shops immerse fans in a sensory experience, creating an emotional connection beyond the product itself.*

Turn Events Into Content Gold: Live-stream, document, and share the energy. Your audience is bigger than just the attendees.

- *Example: Apple's keynote launches generate millions of views worldwide, turning every product release into a global event.*

Lululemon: The Power of Experiential Community Fandom

Want to see **experience-driven fandom in action**? Look no further than **Lululemon**.

This isn't just an apparel brand—it's a movement. Lululemon doesn't just sell leggings; it creates spaces where fans sweat, grow, and connect.

- 4,000+ Events Worldwide—from yoga festivals to meditation retreats, Lululemon has built a global tribe.
- Community Hubs in Stores—not just places to shop, but spaces to work out, refuel, and connect.

- Shared Philosophy—Lululemon's entire brand ethos is about living the experience, not just wearing it.

The result? Fans don't just buy the brand—they live it.

Final Thought: Own The Experience, Win The Fandom

If you're not thinking beyond transactions and looking into immersive, real-world experiences, you're missing the biggest opportunity in fandom today.

- The brands that win are the brands that bring people together.

- The future isn't just digital—it's physical, immersive, and unforgettable.

- Your brand isn't just a product. It's a stage. So what experience are you giving your fans?

The next wave of fandom belongs to the brands that create real-world magic. Will yours be one of them?

Beyond The Hype: Building on Cultural Peaks

Not all fans start as loyal advocates. Some are drawn in by a viral moment, a cultural trend, or a limited-time offer—and may leave just as quickly. But that initial spark is your opportunity. With the right experience and connection, you can turn short-term attention into lasting loyalty.

The Power of Short-Term Fandom

Think about the biggest cultural moments in branding:

- Popeyes' Chicken Sandwich Wars—a frenzy that sold out nationwide in days.

- McDonald's x BTS Meal—a global phenomenon that turned packaging into collectibles.

- Nike's Collabs with Travis Scott or Off-White—drops so exclusive that resale prices skyrocket.

These moments attract millions of transient fans who engage intensely—but temporarily. But what if brands could turn that short-lived obsession into a long-term connection? That's the challenge—and the ultimate opportunity.

How to Convert Transient Fans Into Long-Term Supporters

1. Create Urgency—But Don't Stop There

Yes, exclusivity and limited-time offers generate buzz. But how do you keep the energy going once the campaign ends?

- Example: Nike doesn't just drop sneakers—they keep fans engaged with SNKRS app access, storytelling, and future drops.

2. Make the Experience Unforgettable

If a transient fan interacts with your brand **once**, make sure it's an experience they'll never forget. Even if they arrived for a single moment, leave them wanting more.

- *Example: Disney's 100th-anniversary celebration wasn't just a campaign—it was a spectacle, ensuring that casual fans left feeling emotionally invested.*

3. Leverage Influencers & Trends for Continued Engagement

Transient fandom is fueled by cultural moments. Align with the right voices, platforms, and movements to keep the momentum alive.

- *Example: TikTok trends often create transient fandoms. The brands that win don't just ride the trend—they shape the next one.*

4. Follow Up, Surprise & Delight

Once the moment passes, don't let the conversation end. Follow up with exclusive content, personalized engagement, or loyalty perks that turn a casual fan into a repeat customer.

- *Example: McDonald's turned their BTS collab into a fan-driven ecosystem, extending engagement far beyond the campaign.*

Why Fandom Is the Most Powerful Brand Strategy Today

Fandom isn't a trend—it's the future of brand building. Whether you're tapping into niche communities, nostalgic connections, cultural moments, or subcultures, fandom is how brands move from being seen to being *chosen.*

It goes beyond loyalty—fandom is built on trust, belief, and emotional connection. In a marketplace overloaded with options, it's what makes people not just notice your brand, but stick with it, advocate for it, and defend it.

As someone who has led brand strategy across some of the world's most culturally influential companies, I've seen one truth hold across every market and every audience: when people feel like they *belong* to your brand, you've built something that competitors can't replicate.

Fandom isn't a marketing tactic. It's your most durable competitive advantage.

CHAPTER 4
BUILT TO BELONG.
WHY FANDOM IS THE FUTURE OF BRAND GROWTH.

Marketing is simple. Building a brand is possible. Becoming a Winning Brand that shapes culture? That takes a labor of love and relentless commitment.

So, how do you engage in marketing and branding if you're launching a company in 2025? Or, if you're already established, how do you reposition your brand to not just compete, but to thrive in a global arena teeming with iconic brands—many of which extend beyond your industry? Because at the end of the day, we are all competing for the same thing: attention.

Ensuring that your marketing efforts drive brand awareness, consideration, and full-funnel conversions while delivering a strong ROI is crucial. However, focusing solely on metrics and KPIs is not where great brands begin.

Think about the flood of marketing emails and promotional offers you receive daily. How many do you actually engage with? How often do you simply delete them or scroll past them without a second thought? Exactly. Most of the time.

People don't want to be treated as just another lead in a sales funnel. They crave genuine connection. They want purpose and passion. They may be interested in your products or services, but what they truly desire is to belong—to be part of something bigger than just a transactional exchange. They want a relationship with your brand that is lasting, meaningful, and reciprocal. They want their voice to matter.

It's not enough for customers to know you care; they need to feel it. More importantly, they want to participate in what you're building. They want to love what you do—not just as consumers, but as engaged members of your brand's world. And when they do, you won't just have customers—you'll have fans. And with fans, the possibilities are limitless.

So, how do you build fandom? It starts with cultivating authentic relationships. Fandom isn't about pushing a product—it's about understanding your audience's values, motivations, and aspirations, and then aligning with them. It's about putting their needs, desires, and passions at the heart of your brand experience.

Make no mistake—profitability and revenue are the lifeblood of any business. But when you build a strong emotional connection with your audience, sales and revenue become the natural byproducts of that relationship. As David Meerman Scott puts it, companies that master this aren't just building a customer base; they're building a *Fanocracy*[17]—a movement of loyal supporters who are personally invested in the brand's success.

Fandom is more than just a marketing strategy—it's a transformational force that turns casual buyers into devoted advocates. So, let's dive into how building fandom can revolutionize your brand and create an unstoppable community of true believers.

From Buyers to Believers:
How Fandom Fuels Brand Loyalty and Retention

One of the most powerful advantages of building a fandom is the transformation of customers into a loyal community of brand advocates. These fans do more than just buy your products—they actively promote them, passionately endorsing your brand in ways that traditional marketing simply cannot replicate. They don't just consume; they champion. They share their enthusiasm, recommend your brand to others, and, in doing so, become an invaluable force for organic growth.

When customers evolve into brand evangelists, your marketing efforts become more than just advertisements—they become conversations, relationships, and movements that sustain long-term loyalty and retention.

Cultivating a Tribe of Advocates

One of the most significant benefits of creating a fandom is the transformation of customers into a community of fans who voluntarily act as brand ambassadors. These fans go beyond

---

[17] https://www.davidmeermanscott.com/blog/benefits-of-fandom

mere consumption; they passionately endorse your products or services, becoming brand evangelists who drive organic growth in a way that traditional marketing campaigns simply cannot replicate. Their enthusiasm is infectious, their advocacy is authentic, and their influence extends far beyond any ad campaign or influencer partnership.

This power stems from the deep sense of community that fandoms create. When individuals feel like they belong to a larger group that shares their values and passions, their connection to the brand shifts from transactional to emotional. This emotional bond fosters a sense of pride, making fans more likely to remain loyal, even when faced with competitive alternatives or, at times, a less-than-perfect product release.

And here's the kicker: Emotional engagement often outweighs price sensitivity, creating an almost impenetrable barrier to competitors. That $300 sweater at Nordstrom? No hesitation. That $4,000 MacBook at the Apple Store? Absolutely, count me in. Why? Because when people feel a strong emotional connection to a brand and its community, they don't just buy products—they buy identity, belonging, and a sense of purpose.

Apple has lots of true fans, spending nights in the cold for a new iPhone. Photo by Getty Images.

Just look at sports fans. Diehard supporters don't just follow a team; they live and breathe its culture. They take immense pride in their knowledge—memorizing statistics, debating player histories, and analyzing team strategies—not only to showcase their dedication but also as a form of social currency. Within their fan communities, expertise translates to status. The more you know, the higher you rank in the informal hierarchy of fandom.

This desire for belonging and recognition naturally leads some fans to step into leadership roles. They organize watch parties, manage fantasy leagues, and run fan clubs—not just for influence but because these roles provide a deeper sense of identity, purpose, and connection. Leadership within fandom isn't about authority for authority's sake; it's about shaping culture, fostering inclusivity, and strengthening the bonds between members.

Closely linked to leadership is the value of influence and social status. But fandom isn't just about admiration within peer groups; it's about validation from the brand itself. Fans don't want to feel like passive consumers or targets for marketing—they want to be seen, heard, and valued as part of the brand's story.

That's why status-seeking behavior is so prevalent in fan communities. Those who predict game outcomes with accuracy, offer expert analysis, or curate rare memorabilia collections earn respect and recognition. And in the digital age, this extends far beyond in-person interactions. Fans actively share their opinions on social media, not just for engagement, but to build credibility, grow their influence, and solidify their standing within the community.

The more brands acknowledge, amplify, and empower these voices, the deeper the emotional connection between fan and brand becomes. When fans feel like they are an integral part of something greater, their loyalty is no longer just a preference—it becomes a fundamental part of their identity. And that is what separates a customer from a lifelong fan.

Building a strong fandom can significantly enhance your business by creating higher exit barriers through amplified word-of-mouth, brand evangelism, and trusted key opinion leaders.

Stronger Exit Barriers to Competitors

A dedicated fan base acts as a protective shield against competitors. Emotionally invested fans are less likely to be swayed by rival offerings, ensuring customer retention and enhancing the perceived value of your products or services. For instance, Apple has maintained a customer retention rate of over 90% for the past three years, demonstrating the power of a loyal customer base[18].

Amplified Word-of-Mouth Marketing

Enthusiastic fans naturally share their positive experiences, leading to organic promotion that is both cost-effective and impactful. This genuine passion can attract new customers who trust personal recommendations over traditional advertisements. Companies with strong brand loyalty grow revenue 2.5 times faster than their industry peers, highlighting the financial benefits of cultivating a devoted fan base.

Fans as Brand Evangelists

Fans often become ambassadors for your brand, passionately endorsing your products or services to others. This voluntary advocacy generates organic growth that traditional marketing campaigns cannot replicate. For example, 84% of iPhone owners plan to purchase another Apple device to replace their current one, illustrating the effectiveness of fan-driven promotion[19].

By fostering a community of passionate fans, your brand can achieve sustained growth and resilience in a competitive market.

How Airbnb Builds Devoted Fans

A strong fandom doesn't just insulate your brand from competitors—it becomes your most powerful marketing engine. Fans aren't just customers; they're your most credible marketers, promoting your brand not because they're paid to, but because they genuinely believe in it. Their enthusiasm is contagious, and their advocacy carries more influence than any ad campaign ever could.

Consider Airbnb's strategic shift during the COVID-19 pandemic. Recognizing the limitations of performance marketing, Airbnb's Chief Marketing Officer, Hiroki Asai, emphasized the importance of returning to the brand's core values. He stated that Airbnb

---

[18] https://www.businessdasher.com/apple-statistics/#:~:text=Apple%20has%20maintained%20a%20customer,%25%20trade%2Din%20b rand%20loyalty

[19] https://www.businessdasher.com/apple-statistics/#:~:text=Apple%20has%20maintained%20a%20customer,%25%20trade%2Din%20b rand%20loyalty

needed to "go back to the core of what Airbnb was about – which is about core hosts, primary homes and guests."[20] This pivot involved reducing investment in performance marketing and focusing on big, bold brand campaigns that highlighted the unique experiences offered by Airbnb hosts.

This approach not only reinforced Airbnb's brand identity but also empowered its community to share their authentic experiences, effectively becoming the brand's most passionate evangelists. By investing in the community and showcasing genuine stories, Airbnb transformed its users into advocates who willingly spread the word, creating a ripple effect that no traditional advertising campaign could achieve.

So, before investing a significant amount of your marketing budget in performance marketing campaigns, consider redirecting that budget into exclusive fan experiences, insider access, and engagement-driven moments that money can't buy. The brands that thrive don't just acquire customers; they cultivate insiders—people who feel personally connected to the brand's story. And when fans feel valued, they become your most relentless evangelists.

Brand evangelism isn't passive—it's a self-sustaining, exponential force. Whether through social media, word-of-mouth, online communities, or real-world interactions, fans don't just buy—they recruit. They debate, defend, and influence others to join in.

That's how fandom becomes a competitive advantage—it generates organic marketing at scale and builds exit barriers that competitors can't break. Because at the highest level of fandom, leaving a brand isn't just about switching products—it's about walking away from an identity, a community, and a movement.

And that's when you know you've built something unshakable.

Stronger Community Engagement

When fans feel a deep connection to your brand, they stop seeing themselves as just customers. Instead, they become part of a larger movement—a story they actively want to be part of. This emotional bond makes them more loyal, engaged, and eager to participate in your brand's success.

---

[20] https://www.thedrum.com/news/2023/08/24/airbnb-cmo-ditching-performance-marketing-big-bold-brand-campaigns

Kevin Kelly, Founding Editor of *Wired* Magazine, put it best back in 2008: *"In the era of scaling and mass production, it is rare for a customer to feel a personal connection to a brand. But if you can create just that, surely that customer will feel special. It's like the barista knowing your name when you walk in: it makes you feel recognized, valued, and more likely to return."*

Kelly's *1000 True Fans* theory underscores the power of direct relationships. He suggests that to build lasting brand loyalty, companies must engage personally with their fans—respond to them directly, offer exclusive access, or reward them with limited-edition experiences. Whether it's a personalized message, a surprise gift, or an intimate "Ask Me Anything" session, these small but meaningful interactions create an authentic connection that fosters trust and long-term brand value. Building a two-way relationship with fans isn't just good marketing—it's what turns casual buyers into lifelong advocates, making them true fans[21].

Fans, Community, and Brand Growth

Fandoms thrive on shared experiences, creating strong connections between fans and deepening their loyalty to your brand. Whether it's sports fans rallying together in a packed stadium or Apple enthusiasts bonding over the latest product launch, these collective moments turn customers into a community.

Beyond connection, engaged fans offer invaluable feedback that helps brands evolve. Their insights drive innovation, improve products, and enhance overall satisfaction. When fans feel heard and involved, their loyalty strengthens—not just to the brand, but to the shared experience it represents.

Gen Z's Multi-Screen Engagement

Gen Z has redefined what it means to be a fan. As digital natives, practically born with mobile devices in their hands, they engage with brands in ways that are immersive, multi-dimensional, and hyper-connected. They seamlessly interact with content across multiple screens, spending hours or even days fully immersed in a brand's ecosystem. To resonate with this generation, brands must create experiences that foster prolonged engagement, encourage active participation, and provide seamless digital-to-physical integration.

---

[21] https://medium.com/@jeroenrs/one-thousand-true-fans-all-you-need-to-know-about-marketing-in-a-single-article-fdc3c4cef186

And let's be clear—Gen Z is **not** a niche audience. They already make up **25% of the global population**[22], and by **2030, they will comprise 30% of the global workforce**[23]. Their economic influence is growing at an unprecedented rate, with their **spending power projected to reach $12 trillion globally by 2030**. This generation isn't just shaping the future—they *are* the future. Adapt or get left behind—because Gen Z isn't waiting for brands to catch up. They're building the future of fandom with or without you.

Intel Extreme Masters Pro Tour in Cologne, Germany

Gen Z, the Creator Economy, and the Rise of Winning Brands

Gen Z isn't just consuming content—they're building brands, businesses, and entire economies around their personal influence. This generation has fundamentally reshaped the creator economy, turning passion into profit and followers into customers. The D'Amelio

---

family is one of the clearest examples of this shift, demonstrating just how powerful personal brands have become.

What started as dance videos on TikTok in 2019 quickly evolved into a multi-million-dollar empire. Charli and Dixie D'Amelio's authentic, relatable content attracted massive audiences, leading to brand partnerships with Prada, Hollister, Dunkin', and Amazon. By 2021, Charli earned $17.5 million and Dixie $10 million through brand deals, proving that individuals can now rival traditional corporations in influence and revenue[24].

This shift isn't just about viral fame—it's about power. The rise of creators has disrupted traditional marketing, flipping the script on who controls the direct-to-consumer relationship. Brands no longer dictate culture; creators do. And consumers trust people more than corporations.

According to Yahoo, the Kardashian empire is now worth $1.4 billion—a testament to the fact that individual personalities can command more consumer trust than legacy brands. At the same time, the creator-driven market for personalized brands and products is projected to grow from $230 billion to more than $320 billion by 2025. The ability for creators to sell direct-to-consumer, bypassing traditional retail and e-commerce models, is fueling this explosive growth.

With this disruption comes a question every brand needs to answer: What is your role in the creator economy?

The truth is, that brands can no longer afford to stand on the sidelines. The companies that will win are those that embrace creators—not as one-off marketing tools, but as co-creators of culture. The last two years have forced brands to rethink their place in people's lives, shifting from transactional loyalty to something deeper: human connection.

Consumers today want brands that share their values, integrate into their communities, and speak their language. It's no longer about chasing status—it's about fostering relationships. The brands that thrive will be those that act, think, and engage like people, embedding themselves into the lifestyles of their audience.

---

[24] https://www.marketingdive.com/news/how-an-empowered-creator-economy-is-challenging-marketers/632044/

The D'Amelio sisters, the Kardashians, and countless rising creators have already proven this model. Now, it's up to brands to catch up. The future belongs to those who can move beyond selling products and start building movements, culture, and community.

Enhanced Brand Advocacy and Influencer Power

As fans deepen their connection with your brand, many naturally evolve into advocates, content creators, and even influencers. These individuals don't just buy your products—they actively promote them, using their own platforms like social media, blogs, or podcasts to amplify your brand's reach.

And here's the kicker: your fans have their own fans.

Fandom isn't just a one-way relationship; it's an interconnected web of influence where devoted supporters create their own mini-economies—generating content, sharing recommendations, and fueling demand without the brand lifting a finger.

This phenomenon is tied to the rise of the "fantrepreneur"—fans who monetize their passion by designing merchandise, curating content, or leading online communities. Scholars have long described fandom as a "gift culture," where fans contribute to their communities out of love rather than profit. But that's changing—fandom is now a data-driven, multi-billion dollar economy, filled with influencers, designers, and professional cosplayers who have turned their fandom into a business[25].

This shift demands a new mindset: brands no longer own the narrative—fans do. And when brands recognize, support, and collaborate with their most passionate advocates, they unlock an entirely new level of influence.

This brings us to the next game-changer: leveraging the right voices to humanize your brand.

Leveraging Authentic Voices to Humanize Your Brand

It's time to shift from campaigns to conversations.

People are tired of being sold to. They don't want brands shouting at them through ads—they want brands they can discover, connect with, and trust on their own terms. In a world of over-communication and AI-driven messaging, people crave real human interaction.

---

[25] https://nicollelamerichs.com/2019/03/14/how-do-you-create-fans/

If your brand still operates like a machine—pumping out endless campaigns and impersonal promotions—you're on the verge of losing relevance. Today's consumers expect more. They want brands that engage in meaningful, two-way relationships. Brands that don't just push products but foster connection, purpose, and community.

The good news? Your brand is already made up of people.

Your employees, customers, and industry experts are your most valuable storytellers—and they're ready to advocate for your brand if you let them. By amplifying authentic voices, you humanize your brand, build trust, and create a sense of belonging that keeps people engaged.

But here's the key: Not all voices carry the same weight.

The Voices That Matter

It's not enough to pay an influencer to talk about your product. If the partnership feels forced, consumers will see right through it. The goal isn't just visibility—it's credibility, cultural relevance, and emotional impact.

The right voices can elevate your brand by shaping perceptions, strengthening loyalty, and creating organic momentum. But finding these voices requires more than just picking people with big follower counts—it's about strategic alignment.

The Three Archetypes of Key Opinion Leaders

To maximize impact, brands should tap into **a mix of different voices**, each serving a distinct role:

1. High-Impact Ambassadors – The Rock Stars

    These are your celebrities, athletes, and industry icons. They bring instant visibility and prestige. *Example: Lewis Hamilton Lululemon's endorsements elevated the brand.*

2. Innovators – The Trendsetters

    These rising stars are shaping trends before they hit the mainstream. They offer fresh perspectives, cultural relevance, and influence over early adopters. *Example: A creator known for discovering the "next big thing" introducing your product to a trend-hungry audience.*

3. Grassroots Voices – The Community Builders

These are your micro-influencers and niche leaders with highly engaged audiences. Their authenticity and direct interaction create a strong, trust-based connection with consumers. *Example: A respected fitness coach endorsing a wellness product in a way that feels natural, not transactional.*

Selecting the Right Voices for Your Brand

Beyond their level of influence, the best brand advocates **embody** certain qualities:

- Brand Fit: They genuinely align with your brand's values.
- Credibility: They are respected in their space and influence consumer decisions.
- Style Leadership: They set trends and disrupt the status quo.
- Resonance: They engage deeply and act with purpose.
- Relevance: They are accessible, relatable, and use your product authentically.

A balanced mix of these voices gives your brand the best of both worlds—star power for visibility, grassroots advocates for trust, and innovators for cultural relevance.

The Power of Storytelling Through the Right Voices

The final, and most critical piece? Authenticity.

Consumers shouldn't feel like an influencer is reading a script. The best brand collaborations feel organic, like a natural extension of their personal story.

Brands that integrate the right voices into real, engaging storytelling don't just sell—they build tribes, shape culture, and create lifelong fans.

It's time to stop chasing empty impressions and start building real influence—one authentic connection at a time.

Breaking the Social Media Code: A Strategic Approach for Brand Leaders

What Should I Do on Social Media?

This is the most common question I get asked—from students, my team, and even the executive leadership team. Social media today is what traditional advertising was in the 1990s: if you're not present, you're not in the conversation. The difference? Digital platforms give you the power to weaponize data, track every dollar spent, and optimize engagement like never before.

Yet, despite this potential, most brands are still spraying and praying—pumping out content aimlessly, hoping something sticks. That's not a strategy; that's desperation.

Let's fix that.

The Social Media Dilemma: Where Do You Belong?

Most brands want to know the "best" platform to connect with consumers. Spoiler alert: there isn't one. It's shocking how many businesses scramble to figure out their social media playbook, blindly chasing trends without understanding where their audience actually is.

I hear questions like:

- "What should we do on Instagram?"
- "Should we be on TikTok?"
- "Is LinkedIn the right place for us?"

My answer? It depends.

Before you post a single thing, ask yourself two fundamental questions:

1. Do you know who your consumer is?
2. Are you showing up where they are?

If you can't confidently answer those, then your first priority isn't content—it's learning everything you can about your audience before choosing a platform.

There's No One-Size-Fits-All in Social Media

The key to building a sustainable brand on social media is becoming personal—at scale. You don't just blast content everywhere and hope for results. You tailor your message, your platform, and your engagement to the people who actually care.

Here's how you start:

Know Your Consumer Inside Out

Before you hit "publish," answer these three questions:

1. What are the three most important insights about your audience?
2. What are their dreams, fears, and goals? What's that one thing they'd do anything for?
3. How can you help solve their problems?

Once you nail this, you can map out the barriers preventing them from reaching their goals or simply living their best life. That's your opportunity. Your product, service, or content should either remove those barriers or enable them to succeed.

Finding Your Consumer

If you've done the work, you won't need to guess which platform to use. Your audience will tell you. Are they scrolling TikTok for entertainment? Turning to LinkedIn for career growth? Sharing ideas in WhatsApp groups? Go where they are, speak their language, and build a presence that feels natural—not forced.

This is how you move from just "posting" to creating a scalable, personal connection with your audience. No more aimless content. No more guesswork. Just smart, intentional brand-building.

Amplifying Reach Through Social Media

Social media is a powerful amplifier. When fans share their enthusiasm—through posts, shares, and endorsements—your brand gains visibility far beyond what paid advertising can achieve. The key? Meet fans where they are, speak their language, and create content they actually want to engage with.

How to Create Content That Spreads

- Be Native to the Platform – Content should feel organic, not forced. Each platform has its own culture—respect it. A TikTok trend won't work the same way on LinkedIn, and a polished Instagram reel may feel out of place on Reddit.

- Go Where Trust Is Built – Fans spend time in specific digital spaces. That's where your brand needs to show up—authentically. Share your best content on your website, but also adapt and distribute it to the platforms where fans naturally engage.

- Don't Sell—Entertain, Inspire, or Help – People don't want to be marketed to; they want to connect. Whether through humor, education, or storytelling, the goal is to add value— not make demands.

Post Like a Fan, Not a Marketer[26].

Marketing expert Gary Vaynerchuk outlines what makes content truly native and engaging:

- Seamless Experience – It doesn't interrupt; it blends in.

- Value-Driven – It helps, informs, or entertains instead of pushing a sale.

- Culturally Aware – It taps into what matters to your audience—music, trends, news, and shared passions.

- Snackable & Shareable – Short, digestible, and consistent micro-stories that reflect your brand identity.

Bottom line? Stop marketing. Start engaging. When your content feels like something fans would post themselves, it spreads—effortlessly.

Fandoms:
The Engine for Sustainable Growth

Building a dedicated fanbase fosters sustainable growth for your brand. Loyal fans provide consistent support, creating a stable foundation for expansion, especially in competitive markets with high customer acquisition costs.

---

[26] https://www.sociallysorted.com.au/visual-content-fans-crave/

A prime example is Discord[27], a platform that has experienced significant growth driven by its engaged community. As of 2023, Discord boasts over 200 million monthly active users, a testament to its community-centric approach.

By focusing on user experiences and fostering a sense of belonging, brands can transform customers into loyal advocates. This approach not only enhances customer retention but also reduces reliance on costly marketing strategies, allowing for investment in other critical areas of the business.

Fans as a Brand's Shield in Tough Times

In times of crisis or market downturns, a loyal fan base can act as a stabilizing force. Unlike casual customers who may jump ship at the first sign of trouble, devoted fans are more likely to stick with your brand, offering support and even defending it in public discourse. Their trust isn't built on a single transaction—it's rooted in a deeper emotional connection that makes them more forgiving of setbacks.

A Built-In Defense Against Competitors

Fans who feel personally connected to a brand don't just prefer it over others—they actively resist switching. This emotional investment creates a powerful barrier to competition, insulating your brand from aggressive discounting, market shifts, and emerging rivals. While competitors scramble for attention, brands with strong fandoms enjoy a built-in customer base that remains loyal despite external pressures.

Resident: Turning Customers Into Fans

Online mattress retailer Resident exemplifies how fandom fuels growth. Steve Ryan, the company's managing director of direct-to-consumer marketing, draws from his background in sports marketing to view customers as fans rather than just buyers. Resident's rapid success stems from its data-driven understanding of customer behavior, allowing it to build more personal and lasting relationships.

Ryan emphasizes that while growth is essential, the real goal is creating advocates and true fans. The challenge? Once customers form an emotional bond with a brand, their expectations

---

[27] https://www.businessofapps.com/data/discord-statistics/

skyrocket. As he puts it, *"If you are a fan of one brand, you are not a fan of another.*[28]*"* This heightened loyalty is both a competitive advantage and a responsibility—brands must consistently deliver on their promises to maintain trust.

Your Strongest PR? Your Community.

When a brand faces controversy or negative press, a strong fan community can be its greatest asset. Rather than letting external narratives define the brand, devoted fans push back, offering testimonials, countering criticism, and reinforcing the brand's positive reputation. This kind of organic advocacy is something money can't buy—and something no competitor can easily replicate.

---

[28] https://www.forbes.com/sites/rogertrapp/2021/12/17/why-businesses-need-to-turn-their-customers-into-fans/

WHICH BRANDS
Have the Most Loyal Customers?

Based on the Top 25 Brand Keys Loyalty Leaders 2019-2023

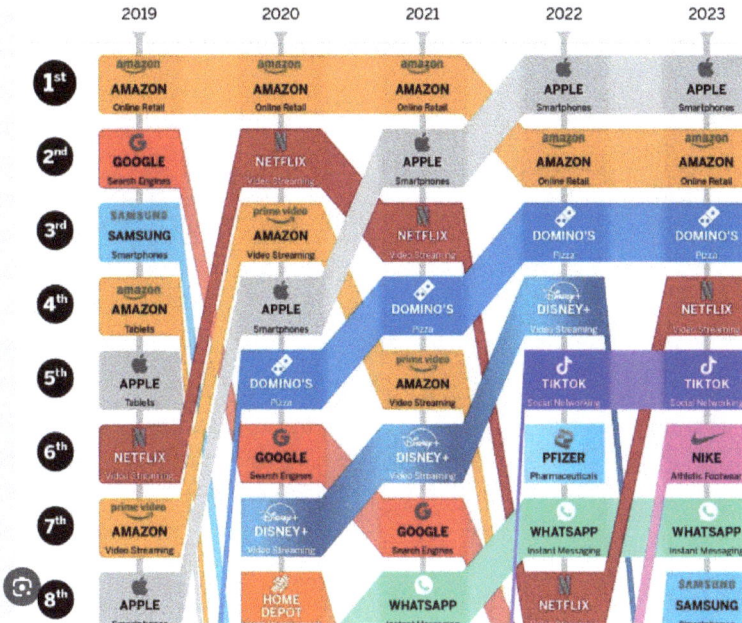

	2019	2020	2021	2022	2023
1st	AMAZON Online Retail	AMAZON Online Retail	AMAZON Online Retail	APPLE Smartphones	APPLE Smartphones
2nd	GOOGLE Search Engines	NETFLIX Video Streaming	APPLE Smartphones	AMAZON Online Retail	AMAZON Online Retail
3rd	SAMSUNG Smartphones	AMAZON Video Streaming	NETFLIX Video Streaming	DOMINO'S Pizza	DOMINO'S Pizza
4th	AMAZON Tablets	APPLE Smartphones	DOMINO'S Pizza	DISNEY+ Video Streaming	NETFLIX Video Streaming
5th	APPLE Tablets	DOMINO'S Pizza	AMAZON Video Streaming	TIKTOK Social Networking	TIKTOK Social Networking
6th	NETFLIX Video Streaming	GOOGLE Search Engines	DISNEY+ Video Streaming	PFIZER Pharmaceuticals	NIKE Athletic Footwear
7th	AMAZON Video Streaming	DISNEY+ Video Streaming	GOOGLE Search Engines	WHATSAPP Instant Messaging	WHATSAPP Instant Messaging
8th	APPLE Smartphones	HOME DEPOT	WHATSAPP Instant Messaging	NETFLIX	SAMSUNG Smartphones

Winning Brands Are Built One Fan at a Time

The power of fandom isn't just about sales—it's about longevity, influence, and connection. A single devoted fan can be with your brand for life. Now imagine multiplying that by thousands, even millions. That's the impact of building a true fandom.

If you want to create this level of brand devotion, start by observing and learning from the best. Look beyond your own industry—analyze how Nike, Apple, and even Doritos cultivate loyal followings. Study cultural fandoms like Game of Thrones or Westworld—how do they sustain excitement and engagement? What do they do to make fans feel like insiders rather than just consumers?

Then, ask yourself:

- How can I apply these strategies to my brand?

- What experiences am I creating for my fans?

- Am I engaging them, recognizing them, and giving them reasons to stay?

Fandom isn't something you build overnight. It's earned, nurtured, and strengthened over time. But when you get it right? It's unstoppable.

CHAPTER 5
FROM LOST TO LOVED. REIGNITING YOUR BRAND'S PURPOSE

Branding is hard. Keeping a brand relevant? Even harder. Many companies struggle to build meaningful and lasting connections with their audience, and if you're reading this, chances are you've felt that challenge firsthand.

Maybe your brand has lost momentum. Maybe customers aren't engaging like they used to. Maybe you're questioning whether your marketing efforts are even resonating at all.

Here's the shift: Stop thinking of your audience as customers and start seeing them as fans. Not in the superficial, "brand allegiance" sense, but in the way people rally around something they truly care about—sports teams, music, communities, causes. Fans don't just buy; they invest emotionally.

Now, imagine your brand as more than just a business. What if it were a cultural movement? What if, instead of just pushing products or services, you were creating an experience people genuinely wanted to be part of?

Your brand isn't just a logo or a tagline—it's the relationship you have with your audience. And when that relationship weakens, the path forward isn't just about better marketing. It's about rebuilding trust, engagement, and purpose.

So how do you take a struggling brand and turn it into something that inspires real connection and loyalty? How do you shift from being just another option in the market to something people actively seek out, talk about, and advocate for?

Assessing the Current State:
Finding the Gaps in Your Brand

The first step in turning your brand around is an honest assessment of where things stand. Even the most well-resourced companies get caught up in the daily grind of campaigns and content, sometimes losing sight of the bigger picture. Brand audits and customer evaluations often take a backseat—until something forces their hand.

Look at the companies that attempt major rebrands only to realize that their audience no longer understands who they are or what they stand for. The best time to refresh your brand is *before* it becomes a crisis. But that requires proactively measuring where you stand.

The Hard Questions: Diagnosing the Problem

Brand struggles don't happen overnight. They build over time—often because companies fail to see the early warning signs. Before you make any changes, you need to ask:

- How does your target audience *actually* perceive your brand?
- Are you delivering on your brand promises, or is there a disconnect?
- What are competitors doing better than you are?
- Is your brand still relevant to your audience's evolving needs?

The Metrics That Matter

To get a clearer picture of your brand's health, track a mix of quantitative and qualitative data. Here are four essential metrics[29]:

- Brand Awareness – Do people know who you are and what you do? This can be measured through surveys, social listening, or brand recall studies.
- Brand Sentiment – What emotions do people attach to your brand? Social listening tools, sentiment analysis, and customer feedback can reveal perception trends.
- Brand Equity – What value does your brand add? This includes perceived quality, trust, and loyalty—all of which impact pricing power and market position.

---

[29] https://www.forbes.com/councils/forbesagencycouncil/2019/02/07/how-to-objectively-evaluate-your-current-brand/

- Brand Relevance – Does your brand still matter to your audience? A high-relevance brand aligns with shifting customer preferences, emerging trends, and cultural movements. If consumers no longer feel your brand is *for them*, you have a relevance problem.

One common tool for measuring brand sentiment is Net Promoter Score (NPS)—a simple yet effective way to gauge customer advocacy. NPS asks customers one key question:

How likely are you to recommend this brand to a friend or colleague?

Responses fall into three categories:

- Promoters (loyal enthusiasts)
- Passives (neutral buyers)
- Detractors (unhappy customers)

Your final NPS score gives you a pulse check on how your audience truly feels about your brand.

Beyond the Numbers: The Story Behind the Data

Metrics alone won't tell you *why* your brand is struggling. Pair them with qualitative insights from:

- Customer interviews and feedback – What do they love? What frustrates them?
- Employee perspectives – How do they see the brand from the inside?
- Competitor analysis – What do other brands do that resonates better?

This mix of hard data and human insights will give you a 360-degree view of your brand's current standing—and more importantly, a roadmap for where to go next.

Tools for Assessment:
Finding the Gaps in Your Brand's Story

Now that you've gathered the big-picture data, it's time to dig deeper. Numbers can tell you *what* is happening, but real insights come from understanding *why*. The best way to do that?

Listen. Not just to the data but to the people behind it—your customers, your employees, and even your competitors' audiences.

How to Gather Real, Actionable Insights

- IRL Focus Groups – Your customers hold the answers. Ask them what they love, what frustrates them, and what would make them more engaged. Keep it real, short, honest, and to the point.

- Social Media Listening – Platforms like Twitter, Instagram, and TikTok are unfiltered focus groups. Pay attention to how people talk about your brand in real conversations— what's working, what's not, and what's being said about competitors.

- Market Research – Who's winning in your space? Why? Analyzing your competitors can reveal gaps in your own strategy and areas where you can stand out.

Red Flags: The Warning Signs Your Brand Needs a Turnaround

Before you can fix the problem, you need to recognize the symptoms. Watch for these:

- Declining Sales Trends – A steady dip in revenue or market share often signals brand fatigue or lost relevance.

- Negative Reviews or Social Media Silence – Are people complaining? Worse, is no one talking about you at all? Engagement is just as important as sentiment.

- High Churn Rates & Low Retention – If customers aren't sticking around, your brand isn't giving them a reason to.

The more of these warning signs you recognize, the clearer your path to change becomes.

From Insights to Action: Setting Measurable Goals

By now, you should have a clear picture of where your brand stands. The next step? Defining *where* you want to go and *how* you'll get there.

- Do you need a full rebrand? If people don't understand who you are or what you stand for, it may be time for a deeper transformation.

- Are you looking to increase brand equity? Strengthening brand perception and emotional connection could be your next priority.

- Is your goal to build a fandom? Of course, it is! But fandom isn't built overnight—it starts with engagement, trust, and giving people a reason to *care* beyond just what you sell.

Pro tip: Your customers will tell you exactly how they feel—if you're willing to listen. Ask them for *the good, the bad, and the ugly*. Then, more importantly, *act* on it. Because knowing what's wrong is only half the battle—fixing it is where brands separate themselves from the pack.

Revisiting Your Brand's Purpose: Why Do You Exist?

Is your company truly differentiating itself, or are you blending into the sea of sameness? If your brand feels lost, it may be because your products, services, or experiences aren't standing out. Maybe you're in the same place Apple was in 1996—struggling for relevance. Or perhaps you're facing the same identity crisis GoPro encountered in 2015, where the excitement faded, and the brand lacked a clear direction forward.

The difference between stagnation and reinvention often comes down to one fundamental question: Why do you exist?

What Is Brand Purpose?

Brand purpose is more than just a mission statement—it's your higher reason for existing beyond profit. It's the heartbeat of your brand, the force that compels customers to choose *you* over another option.

Simon Sinek's now-famous framework, "Start with Why," provides a powerful guide here. Brands that lead with *why*—their deeper purpose—build everything else from that foundation[30]:

- The *"Why"*– Your purpose—your cause or belief—is the reason your brand exists. It's what drives your team, guides your decisions, and gives people a reason to care.
- The *"How"*– Your operations, culture, and brand experience define how you show up—and they're what set you apart in a crowded market.

---

[30] https://simonsinek.com/golden-circle/

- The *"What"* – The products you sell or services you offer are the most tangible expression of your brand's promise. They must consistently deliver value to earn trust and drive loyalty.

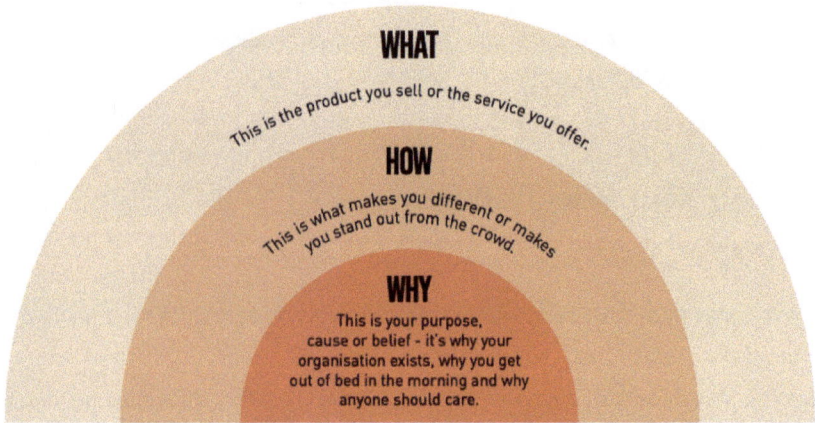

WHAT

This is the product you sell or the service you offer.

HOW

This is what makes you different or makes you stand out from the crowd.

WHY

This is your purpose, cause or belief - it's why your organisation exists, why you get out of bed in the morning and why anyone should care.

BLUEPRINT FOR BUILDING BRAND FANDOM

Purpose as Your Brand's North Star

A brand without a clear purpose is like a ship without a rudder—directionless, at the mercy of the waves. If your brand's momentum has stalled, the first step isn't a marketing overhaul or a flashy rebrand. It's going back to the core reason you exist.

So, ask yourself: Beyond making a profit, what is your brand's purpose?

If you can't answer that clearly, it's time to dig deeper—because the brands that know why are the ones that create movements, not just products.

Defining Your "Why"

Your brand's purpose should serve as its foundation—the guiding force behind everything you do. When a brand is clear on its *why*, it creates stronger emotional connections, aligns internal teams, and fosters deep loyalty among customers.

Key Elements of a Strong Brand Purpose:

- Mission Statement: A clear and compelling mission gives your brand direction. For example, Patagonia's commitment to environmental sustainability sets it apart, making it more than just an outdoor apparel brand—it's a movement.

- Core Values: Revisit what your brand stands for. Are these values actively reflected in your business decisions, culture, and customer interactions?

- Emotional Connection: A purpose-driven brand resonates on a deeper level, forging lasting relationships that go beyond transactions.

One of the best examples of a purpose-driven brand is LEGO Group.

LEGO's mission is simple yet profound:

"To inspire and develop the builders of tomorrow."

Bringing Purpose to Life: The LEGO Group Example

LEGO isn't just selling plastic bricks—it's shaping future generations through creativity, learning, and problem-solving. Its *purpose is embedded* in everything it does, from designing innovative play experiences to fostering STEM education and sustainability initiatives.

- The "Why" – Empowering children to think creatively and develop lifelong learning skills.

- The "How" – Creating engaging, hands-on play experiences that spark imagination and problem-solving.

- The "What" – A diverse range of LEGO sets, educational programs, and partnerships that reinforce its mission.

LEGO's purpose doesn't just attract customers—it inspires them. Parents see LEGO as an investment in their child's development, and employees take pride in working for a company that nurtures creativity.

As LEGO has demonstrated, when a brand's purpose is clear and authentic, it galvanizes employees, attracts passionate customers, and creates a legacy that extends far beyond the products it sells.

So, ask yourself: Is your brand simply selling a product, or is it building something bigger?

Shifting the Narrative:
Rebranding with Purpose and Consistency

Rebranding isn't just about refreshing your logo or tweaking your tagline—it's about *realigning* your brand with your audience in a way that feels both authentic and forward-thinking. The way you communicate your brand story influences how customers perceive you, how they engage with you, and ultimately, how loyal they remain.

But here's the key: Congruence across all touchpoints is critical.

Every piece of your brand—the way it looks, the way it sounds, the way it behaves—must reinforce the same message. This alignment across the **entire marketing mix** (product, price, place, promotion) is what separates strong brands from Winning Brands. When there's a disconnect, customers feel it. When there's congruence, customers trust it.

What Does Congruence Look Like in a Winning Brand?

- Visual Identity – A refreshed logo, color palette, or design isn't just aesthetic; it signals a strategic shift. Apple's minimalist design language, for example, reflects its philosophy of simplicity, innovation, and premium quality.

- Messaging – Your tone of voice, storytelling, and positioning must align with your brand's evolved identity. Dunkin's shift from "Dunkin' Donuts" to just "Dunkin'" reinforced its focus on speed, convenience, and coffee culture.

- Product & Experience – Every touchpoint, from packaging to customer service, must reflect the brand promise. Nike doesn't just sell shoes—it sells motivation, and that ethos is infused in everything from store design to marketing campaigns.

- Marketing Channels & Execution – If your brand stands for sustainability, but uses wasteful manufacturing processes, the inconsistency will hurt your credibility. Patagonia's brand congruence is why it successfully commands loyalty.

Rebranding Done Right: Key Steps

- Start with Your Audience – Customers should feel involved in the evolution of your brand, not blindsided by it. Conduct surveys, test messaging, and ensure you're solving *their* problems.

- Frame the Conversation – A rebrand should shift how audiences think about you. What perception do you need to change? Are you moving from traditional to innovative? From exclusive to accessible?

- Consistency is Non-Negotiable – Every touchpoint should tell the same story. If you update your logo but your customer service still operates like it did ten years ago, the disconnect will dilute the impact of your rebrand.

- Evolve Gradually – Sudden, drastic shifts can alienate your most loyal customers. A phased approach helps customers transition with you.

Branding as a Tool for Narrative Change

A brand isn't just a marketing tool—it's a framing device. It sets the context for how customers, employees, and even competitors see you. The brands that dominate do so because they control the conversation around them.

A brand can set the context and frame the conversation[31].

So, ask yourself:

- Are you dictating your narrative, or is the market-defining it for you?

- Is every element of your brand reinforcing the same message, or are there inconsistencies?

- What will your audience believe about your brand *after* you reposition it?

Because in today's landscape, *perception is reality.* And the brands that master congruence across every touchpoint are the ones that don't just survive change—they lead it.

Segmenting Your Audience:
From Data to Human-Centered Strategy

Understanding your audience isn't just about collecting data—it's about *bringing that data to life* in a way that informs every decision you make. While we've already discussed the importance of knowing your audience, the next step is segmenting them effectively.

---

[31] https://www.hyperakt.com/insights/a-powerful-dose-of-narrative-change

Think of it this way: **You're not just marketing to consumers; you're building for people.**
And the best brands don't just analyze demographics; they *humanize* them.

Why Segmentation Matters

Most brands make the mistake of treating their audience as one monolithic group. However,
customers have different motivations, pain points, and desires. To build a Winning Brand,
you must break your audience down into meaningful segments and create **personas**—semi-
fictional representations of your ideal customers. These personas serve as guides, ensuring
that your brand stays personal, relevant, and human.

How to Segment Your Audience

Instead of relying solely on broad categories like "Millennials" or "Gen Z," develop
actionable audience segments by blending the following:

- Demographics: Age, gender, location, income level, education
- Psychographics: Interests, lifestyle, values, aspirations
- Behavioral Insights: Purchase patterns, engagement trends, brand interactions
- Cultural & Social Identity: Subcultures, niche communities, fandoms they participate in

Consumer Muses: Bringing Your Audience to Life

Winning Brands go beyond data points—they create consumer muses to inspire their work.
Think of consumer muses as more than just personas; they're the emotional heartbeat of your
brand strategy, product creation and messaging.

For example, let's look at how brands use consumer muses:

- Nike's "Everyday Athlete" – Nike doesn't just target top tier athletes. Their brand
  persona includes the weekend warrior, the mom training for her first 5K, and the person
  who just wants to be active and feel good.
- LEGO's "Builder of Tomorrow" – LEGO isn't just for kids—it's for creative minds of
  all ages who see the world as something to be built and rebuilt. This muse influences
  everything from product design to marketing campaigns.

- Airbnb's "Experience-Seeker" – Airbnb doesn't just cater to travelers; it appeals to people who seek immersive, meaningful experiences beyond traditional tourism.

By giving these audience segments *names, stories, and motivations*, you shift from generic marketing to human-centered branding.

How to Build Personas & Consumer Muses

1. Identify Core Segments: Use data to pinpoint your primary customer groups.
2. Assign a Face & Story: Bring each segment to life with a name, a background, and key motivations.
3. Define Their Emotional Triggers: What excites them? What frustrates them? What makes them loyal?
4. Map Their Journey: Understand how they interact with your brand, from discovery to purchase to advocacy. Where do they spend their time? What channels do they use to consume content?

Why This Matters

When you create personas and muses, every brand decision becomes more intentional. Instead of asking, *"What should we do?"* you start asking, *"What would [our muse] love?"*

And that's when your brand stops being a product—and starts being a movement.

Taco Bell's Live Más[32]—Turning Fans into the Face of the Brand

Taco Bell's *Live Más* campaign is a masterclass in leveraging customer feedback and community engagement to revitalize brand identity. Instead of relying on traditional celebrity endorsements, Taco Bell put its own fans at the center of the narrative—quite literally—by featuring nearly 400 real customers in its 2025 Super Bowl ad.

---

[32] https://www.tacobell.com/newsroom/taco-bell-features-nearly-400-real-fans-in-its-big-game-ad

The Challenge: Refreshing Brand Identity

Taco Bell has always had a passionate fanbase, but in a fast-moving QSR (quick-service restaurant) landscape, keeping customers engaged requires more than just new menu items. With shifting consumer preferences and rising competition from brands like Chipotle and Shake Shack, Taco Bell needed to deepen its emotional connection with fans while reinforcing its unique, irreverent brand personality.

The Strategy: Listen, Engage, and Feature Real Fans

Instead of dictating the message, Taco Bell listened to its audience. The brand recognized that its most passionate customers were already engaging with its products in creative ways— whether through social media, user-generated content, or viral trends. The insight? Let the fans tell the story.

For its Super Bowl campaign, Taco Bell took an unconventional route:

- They invited real fans (not actors or influencers) to be part of the commercial.
- The ad featured nearly 400 Taco Bell superfans, including actual customers, longtime brand enthusiasts, and members of the Taco Bell community.
- The spot celebrated the free-spirited energy of Taco Bell's fanbase, reinforcing the *Live Más* ethos.

By shifting the spotlight to its customers, Taco Bell turned its audience into brand ambassadors—empowering them to represent the brand in a way that felt authentic and engaging.

The Impact: Brand Love at Scale

- The campaign generated massive social media engagement, with fans sharing their excitement about being featured in the ad.
- Taco Bell reinforced its position as a brand that listens, engages, and celebrates its community of fans, creating deeper loyalty.
- By making *real* fans the stars, Taco Bell transformed passive consumers into active brand evangelists—a long-term advantage that goes beyond just one campaign.

Key Takeaways for Brand Leaders

Taco Bell's *Live Más* campaign highlights an essential truth: Customers want to be part of the brand story, not just marketed to.

- Engagement Over Advertising: Today's customers crave brands that listen and involve them, not just sell to them.

- Authenticity Wins: Featuring real fans instead of polished influencers or celebrities creates deeper emotional connections.

- Feedback as Fuel: By acknowledging and incorporating audience voices, brands build a community that is invested in their success.

The lesson? Customers aren't just consumers—they're co-creators. When you hand them the mic, they don't just amplify your message; they make it their own.

From Big Ideas to Everyday Application: Where Do You Start?

The Taco Bell *Live Más* campaign was a massive success, a brand leader's dream brought to life. But here's the real question: What comes first—the big idea or the fans?

Many companies fall into the trap of chasing a viral moment without first building a solid foundation of loyal fans. But Taco Bell's ability to execute such a bold campaign wasn't just about a flashy Super Bowl ad—it was built on years of cultivating fandom, listening to its community, and delivering consistently on its brand promise.

So, how do you apply this thinking to your own brand, regardless of size or industry? Let's break it down into something every business can apply immediately: the products and services themselves.

Revamping Your Products or Services: Creating Quality Fans Will Love

A struggling brand often has one common denominator: a subpar product or service. You can have the most engaging marketing in the world, but if your offerings don't meet expectations, no amount of storytelling will save you.

Revitalizing your brand starts with making sure what you're selling is something people *genuinely* want. Not just something that works—but something that excites them, solves their problems and gives them a reason to come back.

The Two Ways to Improve a Product or Service

1. Adding New Features

- This is the splashy route—the one that makes headlines and gets people talking.
- New features expand the product's scope, attracting fresh attention, media coverage, and potentially a new customer base.
- However, this approach is also risky—if the new features don't resonate, they can feel like gimmicks rather than meaningful innovations.

2. Improving Existing Features

- This is where long-term brand strength is built. Enhancing what customers already use makes them more engaged, loyal, and likely to advocate for your brand.

3. Three ways to improve existing features

- Deliberate Improvement: Make an existing feature better.
- Frequency Improvement: Make it easier for customers to use more often.
- Adoption Improvement: Simplify or enhance accessibility so more people can use it.

How Do You Know What to Improve?

It all comes down to listening, observing, and anticipating what will drive deeper engagement.

- Customer Feedback: What are the common frustrations or requests? The loudest complaints often signal the most important opportunities.
- Competitive Analysis: What do your competitors do better than you? Where are they stealing market share, and how can you surpass them?
- Industry Trends: Are you ahead of the curve or falling behind? Innovation is key to long-term brand relevance.

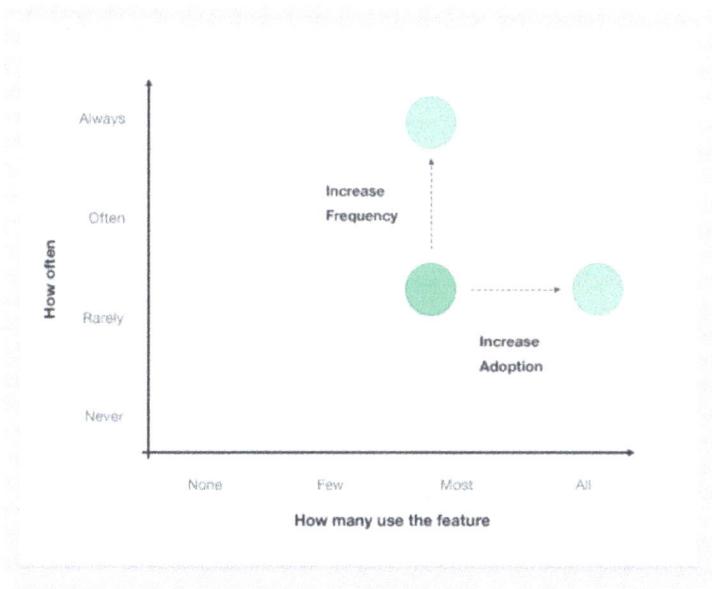

Consistency Over Novelty: The Power of Quality

A great brand isn't built on one big moment. It's built on consistent, high-quality experiences that make fans trust and love what you do.

Take Apple, for example. Every product they release shows a relentless focus on design, user experience, and functionality—ensuring that fans don't just buy their devices, but anticipate the next launch. That level of consistency builds trust, habit, and ultimately, devotion.

The takeaway? Before you chase a big idea, make sure your foundation is rock solid. Because the real magic happens when people aren't just buying a product, but believing in it.

Emotional Connection: The Hidden Growth Engine

Fans don't just buy products—they buy feelings, identity, and connection. They don't just want a transactional relationship with your brand; they want to feel seen, heard, and valued. They crave authenticity, and they can instantly recognize when a brand is simply selling versus genuinely engaging.

In today's hyper-connected world, traditional advertising alone won't cut it. Businesses that focus solely on acquiring new customers will inevitably hit a ceiling. The real long-term growth comes from building emotional connections that foster trust, loyalty, and advocacy.

Why Emotional Connection Matters in Business

Think about the brands you love. The ones that feel like part of your life. Maybe it's the sneakers you always wear, the coffee shop you visit daily, or the technology you can't live without. These aren't just products—they represent something bigger: self-expression, nostalgia, empowerment, or community.

And this isn't just anecdotal—it's backed by data. Companies that cultivate deep emotional connections with their customers see a 51% higher revenue and sales performance compared to those that don't[33]. Why? Because emotional bonds build long-term customer value.

Brands that invest in relationship marketing—connections built on trust, personalization, and mutual understanding—don't just chase one-time purchases; they create lifelong followers who spend more and advocate for the brand.

Long-Term Emotional Impact: Nike's Playbook for Brand Devotion

Few brands understand this better than Nike. Their brand promise—to bring innovation and inspiration to every athlete—has been at the core of their success for decades. But it's not just about making great shoes; it's about making people feel something.

Nike's *Dream Crazy* campaign is a perfect case study of how emotional connection translates into real business results. Featuring Colin Kaepernick, a NFL Quarterback who had been suspended for kneeling during the National Anthem before games, the campaign tapped into powerful themes of perseverance, and social justice. It wasn't just an ad—it was a statement.

The Immediate Impact

- In the days following the campaign's launch, Nike's online sales surged by 31% compared to the previous year.

- The campaign sparked global conversations, dominating news cycles and social media.

---

[33] https://www.hartehanks.com/blog/why-relationship-marketing-matters/

The Long-Term Business Effect

- While Nike's stock price dipped initially due to ad's controversial aspect, it quickly rebounded and ended the year up nearly 18%[34].

- The brand strengthened its relationship with loyal fans who resonated with the campaign's message.

- Instead of playing it safe, Nike deepened its emotional bond with customers, reinforcing its position as a brand that stands for something.

Making It Real: How Brands Can Build Emotional Bonds

1. **Define What You Stand For:** Consumers align with brands that reflect their values. What does your brand *really* believe in?

2. **Speak to Emotion, Not Just Logic:** Nike doesn't say buy our shoes. They say *Just Do It.* They promote inspiration, action and confidence. How does your brand make people feel?

3. **Engage in Meaningful Conversations:** Fans want brands that listen, respond, and interact authentically. What are you doing to engage your audience beyond selling?

4. **Stay Consistent Across All Touchpoints:** Emotional connections aren't built overnight—they're reinforced over time through consistent storytelling, product experience, and engagement.

The Takeaway

A brand without an emotional connection is forgettable. A brand that *moves people* becomes iconic. When you make your audience *feel something*, they don't just buy your product—they buy into your brand. And when that happens, loyalty isn't something you chase—it's something you earn.

Building Brands That People Believe In

Compelling storytelling transforms passive customers into passionate fans. Your brand's story isn't just a marketing asset—it's the foundation of your connection with your audience.

---

[34] https://thebrandhopper.com/2024/09/28/a-case-study-on-nikes-dream-crazy-campaign/

So, what is storytelling in the context of branding? Storytelling is about weaving narratives that make people care—not just about what you sell, but about who you are and why you exist. It's the ability to evoke empathy, spark imagination, and make your audience feel something real.

Seth Godin famously said, **"**Marketing is no longer about the stuff that you make but about the stories you tell." And the data backs this up. A recent study found that 92% of consumers want brands to create ads that feel like a story. Additionally, research from Edelman shows that 63% of consumers remember a brand's story when making a purchase decision. That's the power of narrative—it sticks.

But storytelling isn't just about showcasing a product. It's about crafting an emotional landscape that pulls your audience in, resonates with their experiences, and inspires action. Done right, storytelling makes your brand unforgettable. It shifts your brand from a commodity to a community, from a business to a belief system.

The Core Elements of Meaningful Storytelling

- Authenticity – Share real stories about your brand's journey, struggles, and wins. Consumers can sense when a story is fabricated.

- Relatability – Connect with your audience's values, aspirations, and lived experiences. The more they see themselves in your brand, the deeper they will connect with it.

- Emotion – Evoke powerful feelings—whether it's joy, nostalgia, inspiration, or even a sense of urgency. People may forget facts, but they remember how you made them feel.

Bringing Stories to Life: Formats to Explore

- Blogs & Articles – Thought leadership pieces, behind-the-scenes insights, and customer success stories.

- Videos & Documentaries – Emotionally compelling short films, brand origin stories, or real-life impact features.

- Social Media Campaigns – Bite-sized narratives told through Instagram reels, TikTok videos, or Twitter threads.

Case Study: TOMS – A Story-Driven Brand

TOMS built its brand not just by selling shoes, but by telling a story of impact. Its *"One for One"* campaign was a masterclass in storytelling. Instead of leading with product specs, TOMS led with a mission: *"For every pair of shoes you buy, we give a pair to a child in need."*

That simple, human-centered story created an emotional bond between the brand and its customers. People didn't just buy TOMS shoes—they bought into the idea that their purchase could make a difference. The result? A devoted following that saw TOMS as more than a footwear company—it became a movement.

Your brand's story is its most valuable currency. It's what turns customers into believers, buyers into advocates, and transactions into loyalty. The question is—are you telling a story worth following?

From Fans To Loyal Tribe

Fandoms aren't just about admiration—they're about participation. The strongest brands don't just collect customers; they cultivate communities. And when fans feel a sense of belonging, they don't just buy—they advocate, promote, and defend the brand as if it were their own.

Why Community Is the Ultimate Growth Strategy

If you can turn customers into fans, you may quickly find that your marketing budget doesn't need to grow as fast as your business does. Why? Because fans do the marketing for you.

Passionate fans create organic word-of-mouth campaigns, posting about their experiences, making recommendations, and even defending the brand against criticism. This kind of advocacy is infinitely more powerful than traditional advertising because it's built on trust. People believe people, not companies.

Another benefit? Retention skyrockets. When people find a brand that consistently delivers value and makes them feel seen, they don't just return—they stick around for years. In a competitive market where customer acquisition costs keep rising, nothing is more valuable than a loyal, self-sustaining fan base[35].

Fans Are the Lifeblood of Your Brand—Act Like It

If your brand wants to build a true community, here's what you need to understand about fans:

- Fans Come First – They decide, not you. Listen to them, engage with them, and co-create with them.

- Speak Their Language – Every fanbase has its own culture, inside jokes, and values. Learn them. Use them.

- Tribes, Not Demographics – Fans connect over shared passions, not arbitrary age or income brackets. Find the common threads.

- They Can Smell Inauthenticity – Brands that fake enthusiasm get exposed. Be honest, own your mistakes, and show up consistently.

- Give Them Ownership – The best communities aren't about the brand; they're about the fans. Let them shape the experience.

Example: LEGO Ideas – When Fans Become Creators

LEGO isn't just a toy—it's a movement. And a big reason for that is LEGO Ideas, a platform that turns fans into co-creators.

Here's how it works: Fans design and submit their own LEGO sets. Other fans vote on their favorites. If a design gets enough support, LEGO considers turning it into an official set. If it gets produced, the original creator gets a percentage of the sales.

Why does this matter? Because LEGO isn't just selling bricks; they're selling participation. They've built a system where fans don't just consume the brand—they shape it.

The results speak for themselves:

---

[35] https://www.forbes.com/councils/forbescommunicationscouncil/2020/10/29/how-to-turn-customers-into-fans-and-brand-advocates/

- *Over 2.8 million members*[36] have joined LEGO Ideas, contributing thousands of designs, contributing with 135,000 ideas for LEGO sets.

- Fan-created sets, like the NASA Apollo Saturn V and the Friends Central Perk Cafe, have become massive commercial successes.

- The program has transformed LEGO from a brand into an open-source creative platform, reinforcing deep, lifelong loyalty—rewarding creators with a 1% share of the top-line product's revenue.

The takeaway? The more your fans feel like they're part of something bigger, the more invested they become. When you give fans a real seat at the table, they don't just engage— they evangelize.

From Community to Movement

Community-building isn't about short-term wins; it's about long-term sustainability. The brands that thrive are the ones that understand that their success is directly tied to the strength of their fanbase.

So ask yourself:

- How can I create spaces where fans connect with each other?
- What opportunities am I giving them to contribute to the brand?
- Am I making them feel like insiders—or just customers?

Because at the end of the day, the most successful brands aren't the ones with the biggest marketing budgets. They're the ones with the biggest, most engaged fan communities.

Consistency and Persistence:
Why Brand Transformation Takes Time

Reviving a brand isn't a quick sprint—it's a marathon. Successful transformations require consistency, commitment, and a willingness to stay the course, even when results aren't immediate.

Research from Forbes shows that most rebrands take 12 to 18 months from approval to full execution. And for good reason—brand value contributes an average of 19.5% of a

---

[36] https://www.pcma.org/lego-ideas-community-crowdsourcing/

company's total enterprise value. Rushing the process can be costly, while a thoughtful, well-executed transformation can deliver long-term gains[37].

It's also rare for rebranding timelines to go exactly as planned. Leadership may set ambitious deadlines, but the reality is that most successful rebrands require adjustments along the way to ensure quality, authenticity, and a smooth transition. The key isn't speed—it's precision.

Key Principles for a Successful Brand Turnaround

- Patience: Meaningful change doesn't happen overnight. Celebrate small wins and stay committed.

- Adaptability: Audience feedback will guide your evolution—listen, refine, and pivot as needed.

- Transparency: Keep your community engaged in the process. People support what they feel part of.

The Long Game Pays Off

The most iconic brands weren't built in a day, and neither are their comebacks. **Netflix** famously pivoted from a struggling DVD rental service to a global streaming powerhouse by staying true to its vision while adapting to consumer behavior. It's proof that persistence, strategy, and listening to your audience can turn setbacks into success.

Stay the course. Build with intention. The results will follow.

Chapter Wrap-Up:
From Struggling Brand to Cultural Force

Revitalizing your brand isn't just about fixing problems—it's about redefining your impact. The strongest brands don't just sell; they connect, inspire, and embed themselves into people's lives.

This isn't a one-time strategy—it's a long-term commitment to building relationships, creating belonging, and delivering value beyond transactions. The brands that win aren't just seen; they are felt.

---

[37] https://www.forbes.com/councils/forbesagencycouncil/2023/10/05/how-long-does-it-take-to-successfully-rebrand-a-business/

So, the real question is: *Will your brand fade into the background, or will it become something people believe in?* Because when you commit to the work—when you listen, engage, and lead with authenticity—you don't just build a brand. *You build a movement.*

CHAPTER 6
TRANSFORM THE SCROLL.
HOW BRANDS WIN
THROUGH INTERACTION.

The first question you're probably asking is, **"Why?"**

Why shift to creating experiences when traditional social media posts, stories, and blog articles seem to work just fine? Because experiences are now table stakes in any marketing mix—making it easier to scale production, distribution, and, most importantly, maintain control of the narrative.

Consumer behavior has fundamentally changed. Social media has empowered audiences to voice their opinions to the masses, shifting them from passive recipients of brand messaging to active participants in their favorite brand's story.

Interactive experiences create a *two-way dialogue* where participation drives quality engagement beyond mere CTRs, views, likes, and shares. All data points consistently show that people spend significantly more time engaging with interactive elements.

But this isn't just about engagement—it's about building and nurturing a fandom. Traditional posts aren't enough anymore. Winning the attention game is the most important job to be done—and the competition is fierce. In a crowded landscape, capturing an audience's attention is hard. Keeping it? Even harder.

The shift from static to interactive content has transformed how brands engage with their audiences.

According to the *Content Marketing Institute (CMI)*[38], *79% of marketers* report that interactive content enhances message retention. Additionally, interactive content boosts engagement by 52.6%, proving its effectiveness.

The takeaway? Consumers expect more. If brands want to stand out, they need to move beyond passive storytelling and create experiences that pull audiences in, keep them engaged, and make them feel like they're part of something bigger.

Benefits of Interactive Content

Interactive content offers distinct advantages over static content, making it a game-changer for brands looking to deepen audience engagement and drive meaningful interactions.

- Higher Engagement – Interactive experiences like co-streaming on YouTube, watch parties on Twitch, and AMA (Ask Me Anything) sessions on Discord encourage active participation, leading to longer time spent on content and a stronger emotional connection with your brand.

- Better Data Collection – When users engage with interactive content, they naturally provide insights into their preferences, behaviors, and interests. This data becomes invaluable for refining marketing strategies, improving customer targeting, and optimizing content for higher impact.

- Personalization at Scale – Interactive content enables tailored experiences based on user input. By responding to audience preferences in real time, brands can create highly relevant, personalized content, fostering stronger relationships and boosting conversion rates.

The takeaway? Interactive content isn't just a trend—it's a competitive advantage. It turns passive viewers into active participants, strengthens brand affinity, and provides marketers with richer insights to drive smarter decisions.

---

[38] https://blog.thepublive.com/content/the-shift-from-static-to-interactive-content-4739291

The Evolution of Content:
From Passive Consumption to Active Participation

Brands looking to build fandom today must recognize that the digital landscape has undergone a seismic shift. Gone are the days when fans would passively consume content through traditional media.

Today's fans are not spectators; they are active participants who want to engage, contribute, and immerse themselves in a brand's world.

Fandom isn't just about consumption—it's about co-creation. Giving your community a platform to experience your brand isn't just good marketing; it's an invitation for them to create, promote, and distribute content on your behalf. And that's where the magic happens— your organic reach scales in direct proportion to the size and engagement of your community.

This shift reflects a broader cultural transformation. Modern consumers value experiences over material things, and that preference extends to how they engage with content.

They seek opportunities to collaborate, interact, and co-create. Brands that fail to meet these expectations risk becoming irrelevant as fans naturally gravitate toward those offering immersive, participatory experiences.

Why Fans Crave Interaction: The Power of Participation

At its core, the demand for interactive experiences is rooted in human psychology. Engagement creates emotional connections and a sense of belonging. When fans are invited to participate, they feel valued, heard, and empowered—turning casual followers into passionate advocates.

Experiential, co-created content connects brands to the heart and soul of their fans. And the best part? It doesn't stop at the first interaction—it fuels an ongoing cycle of engagement, creativity, and shared expression.

When fans are actively involved, they don't just consume—they contribute, shaping the brand's narrative in ways that deepen loyalty and keep the relationship alive.

Once you lay the foundation and launch interactive content, your fans will take the reins, amplifying and expanding upon it in ways no traditional marketing campaign ever could.

Their content is often more authentic, impactful, and trusted than anything your marketing team could produce.

Interactive experiences also introduce a sense of novelty and excitement. The unpredictability of real-time engagement, or the thrill of influencing a brand's story, triggers dopamine-driven reward cycles. This deepens emotional bonds, increasing the likelihood that fans will invest their time, money, and loyalty in your brand.

This is no longer optional. Interactive content is a must-have. According to Forbes[39], the number of businesses incorporating interactive content into their marketing strategies doubled between 2023 and 2024. The brands that thrive will be the ones that actively engage, empower, and co-create with their fans—turning them from passive consumers into lifelong brand evangelists.

Beyond Likes and Shares: Redefining Engagement

Engagement metrics have evolved. While likes, shares, and comments can signal visibility, they don't always capture meaningful interaction. Real engagement happens when fans feel like they are part of the brand's journey—not just passive consumers, but active participants shaping its story.

What Meaningful Interaction Looks Like

True engagement isn't measured by vanity metrics; it's defined by the depth of participation. Some of the most impactful interactions include:

- Collaborations – Giving fans opportunities to contribute ideas, vote on creative decisions, or influence product development.
- Co-Creation – Inviting fans to create content, whether through user-generated videos, fan art, or social media takeovers.
- Conversations – Encouraging discussions where fans engage with each other and the brand, fostering a sense of belonging.

---

[39] https://contently.com/2024/10/24/interactive-content-marketing-makes-your-brand-the-life-of-the-digital-party/

These forms of interaction strengthen emotional investment, turning casual customers into loyal advocates and, ultimately, brand builders. When fans feel heard and valued, they don't just buy—they become part of something bigger.

How IKEA[40] Made Fans Part of the Process

IKEA has long understood the power of customer involvement. In early 2018, the Swedish furniture giant took engagement a step further with Co-Create IKEA, a digital platform inviting customers to help shape the future of its products.

This initiative focused on four key areas:

1. Crowdsourcing Ideas – Fans could submit product concepts directly to IKEA.
2. IKEA Bootcamps – Collaborations with entrepreneurs to prototype new innovations.
3. University Partnerships – Working with students to develop fresh design solutions.
4. Innovation Labs – Partnering with external teams to push the boundaries of furniture and home design.

If a fan-submitted idea showed promise, IKEA could license the technology or invest in developing it further. This created a major incentive: fans weren't just customers; they were potential co-creators of the brand's future.

This initiative generated thousands of customer suggestions—many of which led to real-world innovations. For example, IKEA leveraged fan insights to enhance modular furniture designs, making them more adaptable to small urban spaces.

The key takeaway? Brands that invite participation don't just sell products—they create a movement that fans feel personally invested in. When people see their ideas brought to life, their connection to the brand deepens, and their enthusiasm turns into advocacy.

From Engagement to Ownership:
The Next Level of Fandom

IKEA's approach is a prime example of moving beyond traditional engagement. When fans feel a genuine sense of ownership—when their voices help shape the brand's decisions—

---

[40] https://www.braineet.com/blog/co-creation-examples

they don't just interact; they invest. And in an era where attention is the most valuable currency, that level of participation is what separates a brand from a true cultural force.

So the question isn't just how do you get people to engage? It's how do you make them feel like they belong? The answer lies in participation.

Open Source IKEA

IKEA has designed a platform that allows designers—or anyone, really—to add to or modify its furniture. Here are some elements and variations.

Adjustable frame
A frame that allows many different types of objects to be fitted

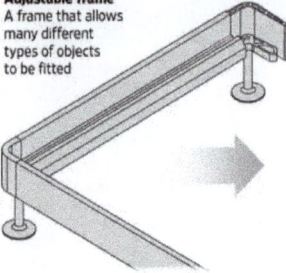

Default kit
Building on an aluminium base, IKEA plans to sell 'snap-on' seats, backs and armrests

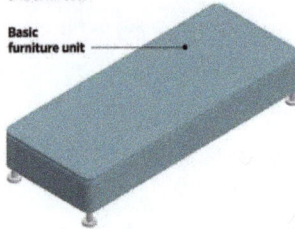

Basic furniture unit

Add-ons
It also plans to sell lamps and side tables that can be mounted onto the base.

Reading lamp

Additional armrests

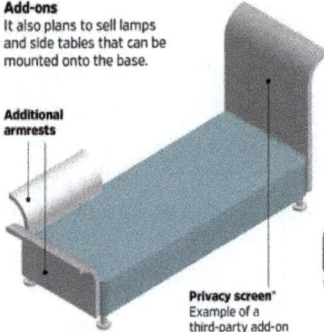

Privacy screen*
Example of a third-party add-on

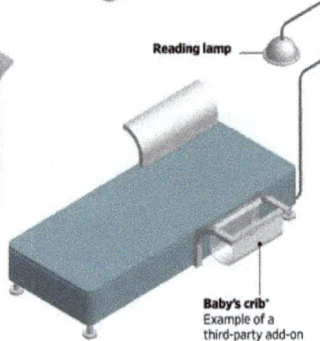

Baby's crib*
Example of a third-party add-on

*Screen and crib were proposed designs from Royal Academy of Art students during an IKEA sponsored workshop
Note: Drawings are approximate and not to scale.   Source: the company   THE WALL STREET JOURNAL.

An example of IKEA's open-source furniture solutions. Source: Harvard Business School

Gamification:
Making Engagement Fun, Habitual, and Rewarding

Gamification is one of the most effective ways to transform passive engagement into active participation. By integrating game mechanics into a brand experience, companies can tap into intrinsic motivators like achievement, competition, and progress—turning everyday interactions into something people *want* to do, not just something they feel they *should* do.

At its core, gamification isn't about *playing games*—it's about designing engagement loops that make participation more rewarding. When done right, it creates a sense of accomplishment, drives habitual use, and strengthens brand loyalty in a way that traditional engagement tactics can't match.

Key Gamification Strategies That Drive Loyalty

- Challenges & Quests – Encourage users to complete tasks, track progress, and earn points or rewards.

- Leaderboards – Introduce friendly competition by showcasing progress among peers.

- Badges & Achievements – Reward milestones, like frequent usage, event attendance, or content sharing.

- Exclusive Rewards – Incentivize participation with discounts, special content, or early access.

By transforming engagement into a rewarding experience, brands can increase participation, build emotional investment, and create an environment where users feel motivated to return.

Headspace[41]:
How Gamification Creates Lasting Behavior Change

A standout example of gamification done right is Headspace, the guided meditation app designed to help people build healthier habits through mindfulness. Meditation is a practice that requires consistency, yet forming a habit around it can be difficult. Headspace removes that friction by incorporating game-like mechanics that make meditation feel easier, more rewarding, and even social.

Here's how Headspace leverages gamification to drive long-term engagement:

- Effortless Onboarding: The app's intuitive start-up process removes hesitation, making users feel immediately at ease.

- Free Entry, Clear Progression: New users get access to free introductory content, gradually unlocking deeper experiences that incentivize paid membership.

- Social Nudges Instead of Leaderboards: Unlike traditional rankings, Headspace subtly encourages participation by showing when a user's "buddies" have meditated. If a friend

---

[41] https://www.beeliked.com/blog/11-gamification-examples

hasn't logged in recently, the app suggests sending them a gentle reminder—turning engagement into a shared experience rather than a competitive one.

- Streaks & Badges for Habit Formation: Users earn streaks and achievement badges for meditating consistently, reinforcing positive behavior through small, rewarding milestones.

The brilliance of Headspace's approach? It doesn't *gamify* just for the sake of it—it uses gamification to enable intrinsic motivation. Instead of external rewards like prizes or discounts, the app reinforces the *habit itself* as the reward.

And that's what great gamification does—it doesn't just entertain users; it helps them build lasting habits.

Designing Engagement: Why Gamification Works Long-Term

When brands integrate interactive, reward-based elements into their user experience, they create something bigger than just engagement—they build long-term emotional investment.

Whether you're encouraging users to take action, rewarding their participation, or creating shared social moments, gamification has the power to make engagement effortless, enjoyable, and—most importantly—repeatable.

Because at the end of the day, the strongest brands aren't the ones with the loudest marketing. They're the ones that make participation feel like second nature.

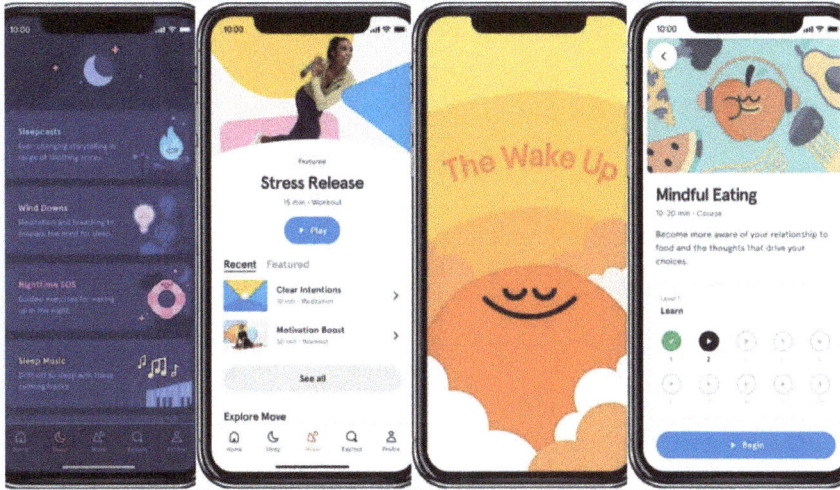

The Headspace app

User-Generated Content: The Ultimate Trust Builder & Community Amplifier

User-generated content (UGC) isn't just a marketing trend—it's the foundation of modern brand engagement. When fans create and share content about a brand, they aren't just promoting it; they're validating it. And in a world where *trust is currency*, nothing carries more weight than real people advocating for your brand on their own terms.

The numbers speak for themselves:

- 60% of consumers say[42] UGC is the most authentic form of brand marketing.
- 50% higher engagement on social media when UGC is included.
- 73% higher click-through rates in email campaigns that feature UGC.
- 80% of consumers say UGC influences their purchasing decisions more than traditional brand messaging.

---

[42] https://www.meltwater.com/en/blog/user-generated-content-examples

Why UGC Works: The Three Pillars of Impact

Authenticity Over Perfection

Fans trust real people over polished campaigns. UGC feels raw, unfiltered, and relatable—qualities that modern consumers actively seek in brands.

Organic Amplification

When fans create content, they share it—expanding your brand's reach far beyond what paid media can accomplish alone. UGC is a built-in distribution network, fueled by passion, not algorithms.

Community-Driven Engagement

UGC turns passive consumers into active participants. When people see their contributions valued by a brand, it strengthens loyalty, deepens emotional connections, and fosters an ongoing cycle of engagement.

How to Fuel a UGC Movement

- Branded Hashtags & Challenges – Encourage fans to share content under a unique hashtag. Think of campaigns like Coca-Cola's *Share a Coke* or Apple's *Shot on iPhone*.

- Photo & Video Contests – Give fans a reason to showcase your brand in creative ways, whether it's an unboxing, product hack, or storytelling challenge.

- Fan Art & Design Showcases – Allow fans to reimagine your brand's identity through artwork, designs, or creative storytelling. LEGO Ideas is a masterclass in fan-driven innovation.

- Customer Stories & Testimonials – Feature real experiences from real people, turning customers into brand advocates and making them part of the narrative.

From Customers to Creators:
The Future of Brand Engagement

The best brands don't just speak to their audience; they co-create with them. The more you invite fans into your brand's world, the more they will shape, share, and elevate it.

This isn't just marketing—it's movement-building.

Because when a brand stops *broadcasting* and starts *collaborating*, fandom isn't just something it nurtures—it's something it earns.

Nike Tiempo VII: Powering the Voices That Matter

In 2017, Nike introduced a major innovation to the Tiempo football boot—the integration of Flyknit mesh with leather, redefining the brand's most iconic boot. With 800,000 units sold into the marketplace, the goal was clear: drive mass consumer adoption and sell through inventory in just three months.

The Challenge

The launch, however, landed between two of Nike Football's most high-profile campaigns—Cristiano Ronaldo's (CR7) and Neymar Jr.'s signature releases. As a result, the majority of marketing investment was reallocated to support those flagship athletes, leaving little to no budget for a traditional Tiempo campaign.

With no media spend, we pivoted to a community-first strategy, tapping into a deeply engaged audience—Bootheads—a global community of football boot collectors, reviewers, and content creators who passionately advocate for the products they love.

The Strategy: Boot Culture Built Through Influence

Our approach was built around co-creation—giving Bootheads the first, exclusive access to the Tiempo VII and letting them organically tell the story.

Here's how we did it:

- Mapped the Top 100 Most Influential Voices in Boot Culture – Identified key opinion leaders with engaged communities across social platforms.
- Created a Limited-Edition Product Drop – Produced only 100 pairs of a special-edition Tiempo VII to generate exclusivity and hype.
- Orchestrated a Premium Seeding Experience – Each influencer received their Tiempo VII as a surprise gift—no briefing, no content requests.
- Scripted the Distribution Timeline – Each delivery was carefully planned, ensuring a seven-day build-up leading to the official launch.

The Results: A Community-Driven Marketing Triumph

Within seven days, the Top 100 Bootheads organically generated:

- 78 million aggregate engagements using the campaign hashtag.
- High-quality user-generated content (UGC)—Instagram Stories, in-feed posts, and detailed product reviews.

With a total marketing spend of just $5,000, covering production, premium packaging, and hand-delivery logistics, we empowered our community to become the driving force behind the Tiempo VII launch.

Quarterly Sell-Through Results: 70% of 800,000 units sold within three months.

For illustration purposes only, using today's retail price of $240.00 for a Nike Tiempo Legend 10 Elite boot:

$$(800,000 \text{ units} \times 70\%) \times \$240 = \$134,000,000 \text{ in revenue.}$$

Why It Worked: Key Takeaways for Brand Leaders

- Exclusivity Creates Demand – The limited-edition Tiempo VII Black Platinum wasn't available for sale, only for collection. This exclusivity built anticipation and desire.

- Gifting, Not Briefing, Builds Authenticity – No influencer was asked to post, review, or promote the product. The unboxing experience, combined with a personalized letter from Ronaldinho, created a genuine moment of surprise and delight—leading to unfiltered, high-impact content.

- Leverage UGC to Drive E-Commerce – Fans flocked to Nike's e-commerce site to purchase the Tiempo VII, where we curated the best UGC from our premium seeding experience, further reinforcing desirability.

- Passionate Communities Are Content Powerhouses – The Bootheads weren't just consumers; they were creators, producers, and editors—delivering better storytelling than any paid ad could achieve.

Final Thoughts

This campaign wasn't just about launching a boot—it was about activating a movement. By prioritizing community over traditional media spend, we transformed product seeding into an interactive experience that delivered measurable business impact.

When you engage the right voices and give them something they truly value, they won't just support your brand—they will amplify it.

Live Experiences:
Real-Time Engagement That Forges Lasting Connections

In today's digital world, where attention spans are shrinking and consumers crave authenticity, live experiences stand out as one of the most powerful ways to foster meaningful engagement. Whether through social media live streams, in-person events, interactive workshops, or exclusive brand pop-ups, live formats offer something that pre-recorded content simply can't: real-time participation and emotional connection.

We see this phenomenon in sports and music all the time (as discussed in Chapter 1)—there's an undeniable energy to being part of something as it happens. The thrill of a live concert, the tension of a game-winning goal, the collective anticipation before an artist drops a new track—these are moments that can't be replicated through static content.

Why Live Experiences Work: The Core Benefits

- Authenticity That Builds Trust – Live interactions strip away the polish of pre-recorded campaigns, making them feel raw, personal, and real. Brands that embrace this format create a stronger sense of transparency and credibility.
- Real-Time Engagement & Feedback – Unlike traditional marketing tactics, live experiences allow brands to respond instantly to fan comments, questions, and reactions—creating a true two-way conversation.

- A Sense of Exclusivity – Live events feel special—they're singular, fleeting, and happen only in the moment. This makes fans feel like they're part of something unique, fostering a *sense of belonging* that enhances brand loyalty.

Brands can leverage live experiences in various ways, including:

- Q&A Sessions & AMAs (Ask Me Anything) – Directly interact with fans, answer their most pressing questions, and strengthen relationships.

- Behind-the-Scenes Access – Offer an insider's look at how products are made, creative processes, or even daily brand operations.

- Product Drops & Announcements – Create hype with **exclusive first-look events** where fans experience new products before anyone else.

- Live Competitions & Interactive Challenges – Encourage real-time participation with contests, voting mechanisms, and audience-driven outcomes.

House of Vans[43]: Bringing Community & Culture to Life

A standout example of how live experiences deepen brand connections comes from Vans, which has successfully turned its House of Vans concept into a physical and cultural hub for its community.

With permanent locations in Brooklyn, Chicago, and London, along with pop-up activations worldwide, House of Vans isn't just a marketing stunt—it's a full-fledged experience designed to bring Vans' core audience together through shared passions like skateboarding, music, and film.

---

[43] https://www.thedrum.com/news/2019/05/22/experiential-marketing-9-examples-brilliant-brand-experiences

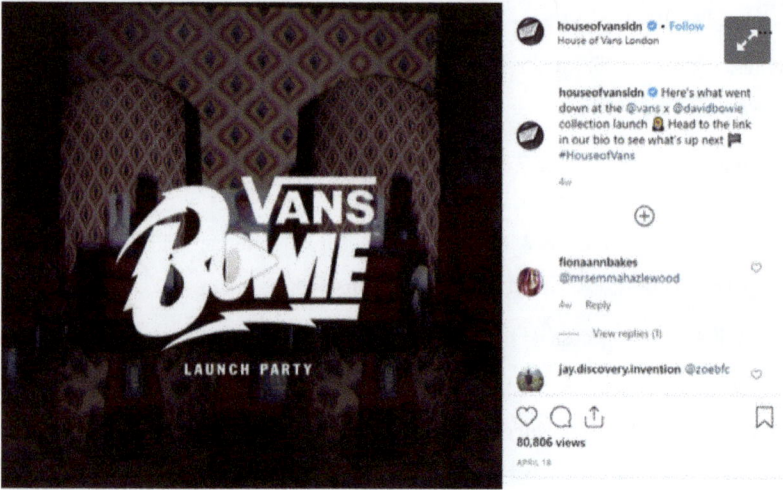

One of the most powerful brand activations took place on International Women's Day when Vans leveraged its House of Vans spaces to champion women in skateboarding. The brand hosted:

- All-female skate sessions – Giving women a dedicated space to showcase their talent and push boundaries.

- Documentary screenings – Highlighting the history and cultural impact of women in skateboarding.

- Live music performances – Blending the lifestyle of skate culture with music, reinforcing Vans' deep roots in both.

This event wasn't just about showcasing products—it was about creating a movement that aligned with Vans' brand values, empowered its community, and gave fans a reason to participate.

The Takeaway: Turning Live Experiences into Fandom

What makes House of Vans so effective isn't just the event itself—it's how the experience connects back to the brand's identity and the fans who shape its culture. Vans isn't just selling shoes; it's facilitating real-world interactions that strengthen brand affinity.

The lesson for any brand? If you want to build lasting loyalty, don't just market to your audience—create experiences that they want to be part of.

Manchester City: Storytelling Through Sports

Sports have always been a powerful medium for storytelling. They evoke emotion, energy, and empowerment, showcasing athletes who push beyond their limits. This is exactly the type of story Manchester City, an English football club with global recognition, told when introducing the top women's goal scorer, Georgia Stanway.

Her story is one of resilience—a woman who overcame adversity to become one of the world's greatest athletes. But it's also a story about a football club that has been deeply committed to supporting women's sports since its inception. In other words, it's the kind of story that resonates not only with dedicated fans but also with those who admire perseverance and progress in sports.

Community Building: Creating Spaces for Fans to Connect and Collaborate

Building a thriving community around your brand is essential for fostering long-term engagement and advocacy. Online communities and forums provide a space for fans to connect with each other, share ideas, and collaborate on projects, turning passive followers into active participants.

Key Elements of Successful Communities

- Accessibility – Platforms should be easy to join and navigate to encourage participation.
- Moderation – A positive and inclusive environment is key to keeping discussions constructive and welcoming.
- Engagement – Brands must actively participate, initiate discussions, and acknowledge contributions to keep the community vibrant.

Popular community-building initiatives include Facebook Groups, Discord servers, and branded forums, all of which allow fans to engage in deeper, more meaningful ways. When executed well, these spaces turn casual followers into dedicated brand advocates.

Personalization: Making Every Fan Feel Seen

Personalization isn't just a trend—it's key to making fans feel valued. When brands tailor content, recommendations, and experiences to individual preferences, they build stronger connections and deepen loyalty.

How to Personalize the Fan Experience:

- Tailored Content – Serve content that aligns with a fan's interests and behaviors.

- Exclusive Access – Offer special perks, discounts, or early access based on engagement.

- Interactive Tools – Use quizzes, polls, and surveys to better understand and adapt to fan preferences.

Fans stay engaged when they feel understood. A brand that **listens, learns, and responds** creates lasting devotion.

Measuring Engagement: Proving the Impact of Interactive Experiences

Tracking engagement isn't about vanity metrics—it's about understanding what truly resonates. To refine interactive strategies, brands must measure impact, not just impressions.

Key Metrics to Track:

- Engagement Rates – Analyze social media interactions (likes, shares, comments, and mentions) to gauge audience participation and content resonance.

- Customer Sentiment & Feedback – Leverage testimonials, reviews, and direct survey responses to assess emotional impact and overall satisfaction.

- Retention & Loyalty – Track repeat purchases, membership renewals, and long-term subscriptions to measure fan commitment over time.

- Net Promoter Score (NPS) – Determine brand advocacy by evaluating how likely fans are to recommend your brand to others.

Leveraging tools like Google Analytics, social media insights, and customer feedback platforms helps brands optimize experiences, refine strategies, and continuously improve engagement.

Practical Steps to Make Interactive Content Work for Your Brand

Shifting to interactive content doesn't have to be overwhelming. Here's a concise, actionable guide to integrate it into your marketing strategy.

1. Know Your Audience & What Engages Them

Before creating interactive content, understand what resonates with your audience.

- Collect Insights: Use surveys, polls, and social listening to identify their preferences.

- Analyze Performance: Look at top-performing content—can it be enhanced with interactivity?

2. Transform Static Content into Interactive Experiences

You don't need to start from scratch—repurpose what you already have.

- Quizzes & Polls: Turn FAQs or insights into engaging, shareable experiences.

- Interactive Infographics & Videos: Add clickable elements to make data storytelling more dynamic.

- Live Q&As & AMAs: Create direct, real-time engagement with your audience.

3. Use the Right Tools for Easy Execution

You don't need a developer—many tools make interactive content accessible.

Easy-to-Use Platforms:

- **T**ypeform & Google Forms $\longrightarrow$ Simple quizzes & surveys

- Canva & Ceros $\longrightarrow$ Interactive infographics

- Instagram & TikTok Live $\longrightarrow$ Real-time engagement

4. Prioritize Design & Usability

Interactive content should be *seamless, intuitive, and mobile-friendly.*

- Keep It Simple: Avoid overly complex features that confuse users.

- Optimize for Mobile: Ensure smooth interaction on all devices.

- Speed Matters: Slow-loading content kills engagement—keep it fast.

5. Distribute & Promote Strategically

Great content means nothing if people don't see it.

Amplify Across Channels:

- Social Media – Drive engagement with teaser clips and interactive posts.

- Email Marketing – Embed interactive elements in newsletters.

- SEO Optimization – Use relevant keywords for organic discoverability.

6. Measure What Matters

Track the real impact of interactive content—not just vanity metrics.

Key Metrics:

- Engagement Rates: Time spent, interaction levels

- Participation: Quiz completions, votes, UGC submissions

- Conversions: Sales, sign-ups, lead generation

7. Iterate & Stay Ahead of Trends

Interactive content is evolving—keep testing and innovating.

- Monitor Emerging Trends: Stay updated on new formats and platforms.

- Experiment & Adapt: Test new features and evolve based on audience feedback.

- Educate Your Team: Keep teams aligned on best practices for interactive marketing.

The future of content isn't passive—it's participatory. Brands that engage, involve, and empower their audience will win long-term loyalty.

FAQs: Making Interactive Content Work for Your Brand[44]

Is interactive content for every business?

- Yes! Every brand can integrate interactive elements, whether it's a quiz, a live session, or a user-driven experience.

What happens if I don't invest in interactive content?

- You risk falling behind. Consumers expect engagement—brands that **fail to adapt** struggle to maintain attention.

How can small businesses use interactive content without big budgets?

- Focus on simple, high-impact formats like polls, surveys, and community-driven content. Engagement > production value.

How do I track the success of interactive content[45]?

- Look at participation, time spent, and conversion rates—not just clicks and views.

Can B2B brands use interactive content?

- Absolutely! Use ROI calculators, industry quizzes, and interactive reports to attract and convert leads.

Chapter Wrap-Up: From Content to Connection

The shift from passive content to interactive experiences isn't just an industry trend—it's a fundamental shift in how brands build relationships with their fans. If you want true fandom, you have to invite participation, create shared experiences, and make people feel like they belong.

---

[44] https://www.linkedin.com/pulse/interacting-future-how-interactive-content-reshaping-viswanath-iabzf

[45] https://contently.com/2024/10/24/interactive-content-marketing-makes-your-brand-the-life-of-the-digital-party/

Brands that embrace interactivity aren't just seen; they are felt. They don't just push messages; they spark conversations. And they don't just have customers; they have a community of raving fans.

That said, static content still has its place. Foundational information, long-form storytelling, and evergreen resources remain critical. The key is balance. Use static content for depth and reliability, and interactive content to drive engagement and emotional connection.

The future of brand storytelling isn't just content creation—it's content participation. Brands that master this shift won't just capture attention—they'll earn devotion.

CHAPTER 7
PARTICIPATION IS POWER. HOW WINNING BRANDS SCALE THROUGH SOCIAL.

Social media is more than just a channel—it's the engine of modern brand-building. It's where communities are formed, movements are sparked, and culture is shaped in real time.

The days of one-way communication are long gone. Today, brands don't just broadcast messages; they engage in conversations, co-create content with their audiences, and cultivate fandoms that transcend borders. This shift from audiences to communities is what separates forgettable brands from those that command lasting loyalty—the Winning Brandss.

The real game? Understanding that social media is not about you—it's about them. The brands that win are the ones that empower people to see themselves in the story, participate in the conversation, and take ownership of the narrative.

But here's the thing—not all platforms are built the same. You don't just "do" social media; you use it with intention. The key is knowing where your audience lives, what drives them to engage, and how to create content that fuels participation instead of just passive consumption.

So, how do you turn your brand into a social-first, community-driven powerhouse? How do you move from being just another account in the feed to becoming a space where people gather, engage, and advocate?

Start with the 'Where,' Not the 'What'

One of the most common mistakes brand leaders make is treating social media as a one-size-fits-all distribution channel. They default to thinking, *What platform should we be on?* Instead of asking the more critical question: *Where are our fans already engaging?*

Social media is not just a megaphone for your brand's message—it's an ecosystem of conversations, culture, and communities. Jumping into a platform without first understanding where your audience naturally gathers is like throwing a party in an empty room. You might have all the right decorations, but if no one's showing up, what's the point?

Here's how to shift your perspective and start with the "where":

1. Map Online Communities – Instead of forcing engagement on a platform just because it's trending, find where your fans are already talking. Are they in niche Reddit threads? Private Discord groups? Specific Instagram hashtags? Your job is to listen before you speak.

2. Identify Cultural Trends – Communities thrive around shared interests, movements, and conversations. Whether it's a viral TikTok trend, a growing subreddit, or a moment in pop culture, knowing what resonates with your audience helps you meet them on their terms.

3. Know Where They Spend Time IRL – Digital behavior is shaped by real-world experiences. Live events, meetups, and conventions provide critical insight into how your audience interacts, what excites them, and where they naturally form connections.

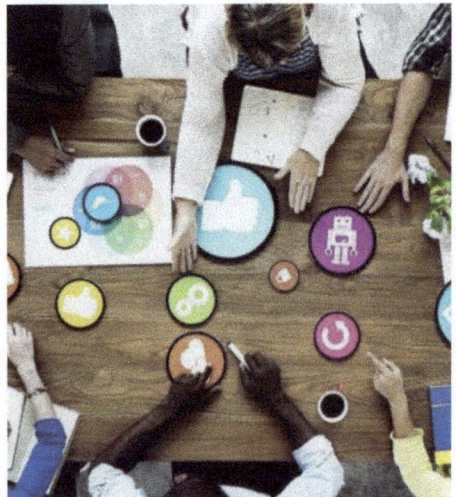

DON'T START WITH THE PLATFORM

TECHNOLOGY MUST ACT AS THE ENABLER OF YOUR BRAND BELIEF, OBSESSION AND MISSION. IT SHOULDN'T BE THE IDEA!

Once you've established *where* your audience is, you can refine your approach by understanding *how* each platform functions:

- Know Where They Are: Dive into audience insights—age, interests, behaviors. What other brands do they follow? What type of content do they engage with most?

- Know How Features Work: Each platform has a different purpose. Instagram thrives on visual storytelling, Twitter is the pulse of real-time conversation, YouTube builds loyalty through long-form content, and Discord fosters deep, community-driven engagement.

- Know Who You Are: Your brand's personality should fit the platform. A playful, fast-moving brand may dominate TikTok, while an esports brand could be more at home on Discord or Reddit. Forced presence on the wrong platform is worse than having no presence at all.

Social media isn't about *communicating where you want your brand to be*—it's about *connecting where your audience already is.* Get that right, and you're not just broadcasting—you're building a community.

Best Practices for Engaging with Fans on Social Media

Engagement is not a passive metric—it's the foundation of fandom. A thriving brand doesn't just talk *to its* audience; it interacts *with* them. Social media is a two-way street, and the brands that win are the ones that show up, listen, and create meaningful dialogue.

Here's how to engage the right way:

- Reliability Builds Trust – Fans need to know when and how to engage with you. A consistent posting schedule creates reliability and keeps your brand top of mind. It's not about volume—it's about showing up with purpose and delivering value every time.

- Lack of Authenticity is a Dealbreaker – Fans can sniff out inauthenticity from a mile away. If your brand sounds robotic, overly polished, or out of touch, they'll disengage—or worse, call you out. Drop the corporate-speak. Be real. Own your story, your wins, and even your mistakes. Transparency builds loyalty.

- Responsiveness Builds Relationships – Social media is not a megaphone—it's a conversation. Answer comments, reply to DMs, and acknowledge your fans. If they take the time to engage with you, show them you're listening. This isn't customer service; this is relationship-building.

- User-Generated Content A Superpower – When fans create content featuring your brand, they're not just engaging; they're advocating. Celebrate them. Reshare their work. When you validate their efforts, you reinforce a sense of belonging—and that's how you turn passive followers into passionate brand ambassadors.

- Interactive Content Sparks Connection – Give fans a reason to engage beyond just liking a post. Polls, quizzes, Q&As, and live streams create moments of participation. The more they engage, the more invested they become in your brand's ecosystem.

Social media success is about establishing deep connection and continuous dialogue with the community. The brands that stand out are the ones that treat their fans like people, not just numbers. The goal isn't just to be seen—it's to be *felt*.

Make Fans Feel Valued

Fandom isn't a one-way street. If you're only broadcasting messages without listening, responding, and engaging, you're missing the point. Fans don't just want to consume content—they want to actively participate in the making of your story. They want to be heard, acknowledged and appreciated.

So, how do you create that sense of connection?

- Ask The Right Questions: Invite opinions, spark discussions, and make your fans feel like their input matters. A fashion brand might let followers vote on upcoming designs, while a gaming company could crowdsource ideas for a new in-game feature. But don't just collect answers—dig into the why behind them. Understanding what drives your audience will give you powerful insights to refine your messaging and offerings.

- Acknowledge Contributions: People remember when a brand takes the time to notice them. Highlighting a fan's content, featuring a loyal customer's story, or simply responding with a thoughtful comment can turn casual followers into lifelong advocates. Recognition breeds engagement.

- Listen & Respond Actively: Pay attention to what fans are saying—not just in your comment section but across the digital ecosystem. Use social listening tools to track trends, identify pain points, and spot opportunities to refine your products, services, or content strategy. The brands that listen best are the brands that win.

- Show Gratitude & Reciprocity: Never underestimate the power of a simple "thank you." Whether it's a direct message, a public shoutout, or a surprise reward, showing appreciation fosters goodwill and strengthens the emotional bond between your brand and its community.

Loyalty isn't built through content alone—it's built through connection. Fans will stick around when they feel valued, and when they do, they won't just engage—they'll advocate.

Turn the Feed Into a Force for Connection

So, here's the challenge: Are you using social media as a megaphone, or are you using it as a conversation? Too many brands fall into the trap of treating social media as a one-way broadcast—a place to push content, rack up impressions, and move on. But real fandom isn't built through passive consumption; it's built through active participation.

If your strategy stops at distribution, you're leaving the most powerful part of social media untapped. The brands that win aren't just seen—they are felt. They create spaces for fans to engage, contribute, and feel part of something bigger than a transaction.

So ask yourself: Is your social strategy designed for visibility, or is it designed for connection? Because the latter is what separates brands that have followers from those that have fanatics.

Going Beyond A Distribution Channel

Social media has the potential to be much more than a content distribution tool—it can be the engine that fuels a thriving, engaged, and loyal community. But that only happens when brands shift from simply broadcasting to truly connecting.

So, how do you go beyond distribution and start building meaningful engagement? It starts with three core pillars: storytelling, community, and authentic collaboration.

1. Focus on Storytelling

Storytelling isn't just a content tactic—it's the heart of brand connection. People don't connect with logos or taglines; they connect with human experiences, struggles, and triumphs.

- Show, don't tell. Bring fans into your world through behind-the-scenes content. How is your product made? Who are the people behind it? What moments shaped your brand?

- Spotlight your fans. Share user-generated content, testimonials, or transformation stories that put your audience at the center. When fans see themselves reflected in your brand, they feel a deeper sense of belonging.

- Make it personal. Founder stories, employee experiences, and fan features all add depth to your brand narrative. Let people see the human side of your brand, not just the polished marketing version.

2. Embrace Community Building

Fandom isn't built in the comments section alone. If you want to turn followers into fans, you need to create spaces where they can engage, connect, and contribute.

- Host conversations, not just campaigns. Platforms like Discord, Twitch, and Twitter Spaces give brands a direct line to their audience. Use them to create real-time interactions, watch parties, and exclusive behind-the-scenes moments.

- Make your fans the main character. Feature their content, amplify their voices, and co-create experiences with them. When fans feel seen and heard, their connection to the brand deepens.

- Facilitate peer-to-peer interaction. The strongest communities thrive when members interact with each other, not just the brand. Encourage discussions, user-led initiatives, and collaborations that go beyond your involvement.

3. Collaborate with Influencers—Authentically

Influencer partnerships can extend your brand's reach, but they need to be rooted in real alignment rather than pure transaction. Today's audiences can easily spot inauthentic sponsorships, and forced collaborations can backfire.

- Partner with the right voices. Choose influencers who genuinely align with your brand's values, culture, and audience—not just those with big followings.

- Let influencers tell the story their way. The best brand partnerships allow creators to integrate your brand into their content naturally. Forced messaging feels like an ad; authentic storytelling feels like a recommendation.

- Prioritize long-term relationships. One-off campaigns don't build trust. Invest in influencers who can grow with your brand and become real advocates over time.

_ PROFILING THE RIGHT VOICES

BRAND FIT	CREDIBILITY	STYLE	CONTEXT	RELEVANCE
· AUTHENTIC AFFINITY WITH YOUR BRAND VALUES · INSPIRATIONAL AND ASPIRATIONAL APPEAL · TRUE CONNECTION, CONSIDER FRIENDS OF THE BRAND	· REFERENCE AND AUTHORITY IN OR OUTSIDE YOUR SPACE · CREDIBILITY THAT BRINGS RELEVANCE FOR THE BRAND · KEY OPINION LEADERS THAT SHAPES CONSUMERS VIEW	· DISTINCTIVE STYLE AND DISRUPTOR IN THE SPACE · RESPECTED FOR TRAILBLAZING · ALWAYS ONE STEP AHEAD, TREND SETTER	· ALIGNED VALUES TO YOUR CORE BELIEF · HIGHLY ENGAGED ACROSS MULTIPLE PLATFORMS · ACT WITH INTEGRITY AND PURPOSE DRIVEN MISSION	· ACCESSIBLE AND ATTAINABLE TO THE BRAND AUDIENCE · ACTIVE USER OF YOUR PRODUCT OR SERVICES · HIGH POTENTIAL FOR EXPONENTIAL GROWTH

HIGH IMPACT	INNOVATORS	GRASSROOTS

The "Spray and Pray" Approach vs. Purposeful Storytelling

Many brands still treat social media like it's the TV of the 2000s—a place to blast messages to the masses and hope they stick. This "spray and pray" approach prioritizes reach over relevance, focusing on impressions rather than impact.

The problem? Reach without resonance doesn't build fandom. Instead of hoping your content finds the right audience, be intentional.

From Push to Pull: Making Social Media a Two-Way Street

- Personalization: Leverage data insights to tailor content to different audience segments. Different fans engage in different ways—make sure you're speaking to them in a way that resonates.

- Interactive Experiences: Move beyond static content and invite participation. Use live Q&A sessions, AMAs (Ask Me Anything), interactive polls, and challenges to create a two-way dialogue.

- Building Relationships: Treat social media as more than a sales channel. Engagement isn't a one-off campaign—it's a long-term strategy. The brands that win are the ones that prioritize trust, conversation, and connection over simple impressions.

Social media isn't just about pushing content—it's about pulling people in.

The strongest brands understand that success isn't measured in clicks and views, but in the strength of the community they build. When fans feel heard, valued, and part of something bigger, they don't just engage—they advocate.

And that's when social media becomes more than a marketing tool—it becomes your most powerful growth engine.

COMMUNITY   DECLARATIVE   PERSONAL

HUMAN CONTENT

VISCERAL   CONTAGIOUS   TRIGGERING

Influencer Marketing:
A Strategic Playbook for Brand Growth

Popularity Doesn't Equal Influence

Let's get something straight: influence isn't about fame—it's about trust. In a world where consumers are more skeptical and time-starved than ever, brands need more than visibility to win. They need connection. And that's where influencer marketing, done right, becomes a strategic advantage.

Unfortunately, too many brands still treat influencer marketing as a glorified endorsement deal—throwing big budgets at celebrities with questionable alignment. If the Kardashians fit your brand and budget, go for it. But only if it's authentic. Influence without authenticity is just noise.

The truth? You don't need a massive budget to succeed. You need the *right* people—those who speak your audience's language, share their values, and can drive real engagement. Because when done intentionally, influencer marketing doesn't just generate impressions— it builds belief.

Why Influencer Marketing Matters Now More Than Ever

Today's marketing has evolved from interruption to interaction. Brands that win understand that advertising is now a form of connective storytelling. In the past, you built up to one big moment—like a Super Bowl spot. Now, it's about *every* moment. The micro-moments that create a personal journey for your consumer.

Influencers play a critical role in that journey. They bring your brand into the everyday conversation—bridging the gap between brand and audience with credibility and personality. As Lindsay Odom put it, "I don't follow brands. I follow people." And that's the mindset of the modern consumer.

In this attention economy, time is the most valuable asset. People have endless options, and they'll disengage at the first sign of friction or inauthenticity. The brands that rise above the noise are the ones that *connect*—seamlessly, meaningfully, and consistently.

So how do you do that?

Here's your 5-step framework to build an influencer marketing program that actually works.

1. Start with the End in Mind

Before choosing an influencer or even brainstorming content, align your goals. Ask yourself:

- What are our brand and business objectives?
- How will an influencer help us reach them?
- What kind of relationship do we want to build?

Don't fall in love with a personality. Fall in love with a purpose. Map influencers to your strategy, reverse engineer the journey, and only then build the plan.

2. Influence Is Currency

The real value of influencer marketing comes from finding the intersection of **context**, **relevance**, and **reach**. That's where true influence lives.

Context x Relevance x Reach = Influence

This formula is your north star. Look for cultural or seasonal moments that matter to your audience—sports, fashion, entertainment—and identify the voices that naturally fit those spaces.

3. Profile the Right Voices

Not all influence is created equal. Use this creative framework to vet the right talent:

- Are they engaging? Do people interact with their content, share it, talk about it?
- Are they trusted? Is there authenticity in how they show up?
- Is their audience active? Look for participation, not just views.
- Do they drive retention? Are people coming back for more?

Your ideal influencer is someone your audience sees as *one of them*, not someone speaking *at* them.

AUDIENCE ENGAGEMENT
RELATE & SHARE
"I SEE MYSELF IN HER"

RECENTLY ACTIVE
BELIEVE IT
"IF SHE CAN, SO CAN I"

WILLING TO PARTICIPATE
TAKE ACTION
"I'M INSPIRED TO DO IT"

AUDIENCE CAPTIVITY
COME BACK FOR MORE
"I CHECK HER IG DAILY"

TAMBOSI
CREATIVE LEADERSHIP

PROFILING

4. Imagine, Identify, Invest

Now comes the creative work. Before reaching out, visualize what success looks like.

- What channels best suit your message?

- What experiences can your influencer help create?

- What does your audience care about right now?

Only after imagining the possibilities should you identify talent that fits—and invest in building a two-way relationship. The most effective partnerships are co-created, not transactional.

THREE STEPS TO ENGAGE WITH INFLUENCERS

IMAGINE
THINK OF INTEGRATED WAYS TO
ELEVATE YOUR KEY INFLUENCERS

IDENTIFY
SELECT INFLUENCERS AND MAP THE
KEY MOMENTS TO BUILD THE JOURNEY

TAMBOSI
CREATIVE LEADERSHIP

BUDGET
BUILD PLAN + SECURE FUNDING FOR THE PROGRAM

5. Build the Integrated Framework

Finally, get tactical. Structure your program like a real campaign:

- Define the budget
- Assign internal roles
- Map the activation journey
- Plan for measurement and iteration

Influencer marketing isn't a one-off tactic—it's a dynamic strategy. When executed well, it gives your brand agility, authenticity, and speed. A strong influencer can cut through silos and connect with consumers directly, on their terms, through trusted voices they already engage with.

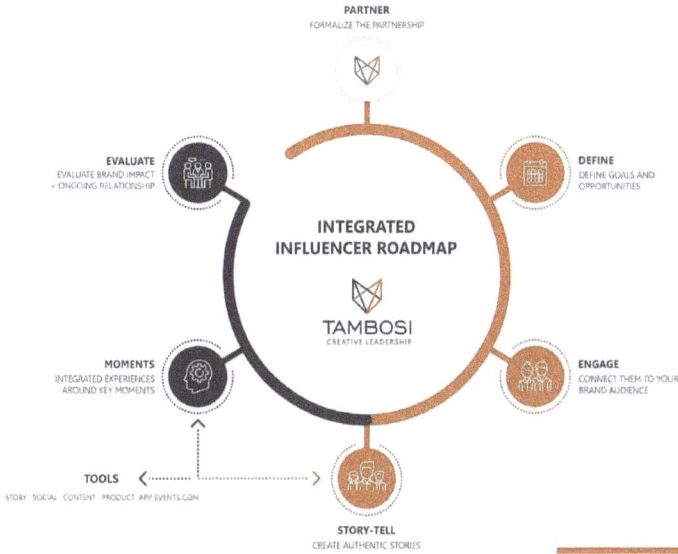

INTEGRATED INFLUENCER ROADMAP

TAMBOSI
CREATIVE LEADERSHIP

PARTNER
FORMALIZE THE PARTNERSHIP

DEFINE
DEFINE GOALS AND OPPORTUNITIES

ENGAGE
CONNECT THEM TO YOUR BRAND AUDIENCE

STORY-TELL
CREATE AUTHENTIC STORIES

TOOLS
STORY SOCIAL CONTENT PRODUCT APP EVENTS.COM

MOMENTS
INTEGRATED EXPERIENCES AROUND KEY MOMENTS

EVALUATE
EVALUATE BRAND IMPACT + ONGOING RELATIONSHIP

Authenticity Is the Real Influence

Influencer marketing isn't a trend—it's a powerful business lever. But it only works when it's rooted in truth. Consumers can smell inauthenticity from a mile away—and they're not shy about calling it out.

Real influence isn't bought. It's built through alignment, trust, and consistent value.

Get this right, and you won't just have reach—you'll have resonance. And in today's world, that's what turns attention into loyalty.

Following the Lead of Influential Content Creators[46]

Influencers and content creators have redefined digital engagement. They've built massive followings not through corporate campaigns or expensive ad buys, but by being *themselves*—sharing their lives, passions, and expertise in ways that feel natural and relatable.

---

[46] https://adage.com/article/opinion/how-brands-can-build-fandoms-and-influence-gen-z-through-social-media/2595246

What's the secret? They don't just broadcast; they connect. They create content that resonates, builds trust, and invites participation—and as a result, they've built fandoms that rival those of major brands.

How Brands Can Build Fandom-Like Influencers

Want to cultivate the same level of loyalty and engagement? **Learn from the best.** Here's how brands can adopt the playbook of successful content creators:

1. Be Transparent, Relatable, and Desirable

Fans don't want polished, corporate messaging—they want authenticity. They want to feel like they're in the loop, discovering products and experiences the same way they would from a friend.

- Drop the marketing-speak. Speak to your audience like a real person, not a press release.
- Show behind-the-scenes moments. Transparency builds trust—let fans see the process, the people, and the passion behind your brand.
- Make it social, not promotional. Fans engage with content that sparks curiosity, emotion, or excitement—not content that feels like a sales pitch.

When brands embrace authenticity, they turn passive consumers into engaged fans who don't just buy—but advocate.

2. Partner with Key Opinion Leaders (KOLs)

Influencers aren't just content creators—they're experts in platform dynamics. They understand how to craft engaging content that blends seamlessly into social feeds, making it feel organic rather than forced.

- Work with KOLs who genuinely align with your brand. Their credibility is their currency—don't dilute it with mismatched partnerships.
- Let them tell the story their way. Overly scripted content falls flat. The best brand integrations feel natural, not staged.
- Think beyond one-off campaigns. Building trust takes time. Long-term partnerships drive deeper connections and sustained engagement.

When done right, influencer collaborations aren't just ads—they're trust accelerators that make your brand more relatable, relevant, and credible.

3. Stay on Top of Trends—But Stay Authentic

Social media moves fast. Brands that stay stagnant get left behind. But jumping on trends just for the sake of it? That's a mistake too.

- Be selective. Not every viral moment is right for your brand. Choose trends that align with your brand's identity and audience.

- Move quickly, but strategically. Trends have a short lifespan. If you're going to participate, act fast—but ensure it feels authentic.

- Create, don't just copy. The best brands don't just hop on trends—they set them. Take inspiration, but bring something unique to the table.

When brands balance trend awareness with authenticity, they stay culturally relevant without feeling like they're trying too hard. The playbook for influencer success is the blueprint for brand success—because brands are no longer the center of the conversation. People are.

Those who listen, engage, and adapt will build communities, not just customer bases. And in today's world, community is everything.

DoorDash x TikTok: Delivering Simplicity, One Trend at a Time

In mid-2024, DoorDash recognized an opportunity to authentically engage with a younger audience by tapping into a viral food trend on TikTok. The trend, popularized by creator Logan Moffitt—known as the "Cucumber Guy"[47]—featured innovative cucumber salad recipes that captivated millions. DoorDash partnered with Moffitt to showcase how effortlessly users could obtain fresh ingredients through their platform, reinforcing their brand promise of "ease of use" and "simplicity."

---

[47] https://adage.com/article/digital-marketing-ad-tech-news/tiktok-cucumber-guy-why-flamingo-and-k18-sponsored-food-videos/2577321

Campaign Strategy

DoorDash collaborated with Moffitt to create content that seamlessly integrated their service into his popular recipe videos. In one notable partnership, Moffitt demonstrated how easy it was to procure all the necessary ingredients for his viral cucumber salad using DoorDash. This approach ensured the content remained relatable and engaging, while subtly highlighting DoorDash's convenience.

The collaboration yielded significant engagement:

- Audience Reach: Moffitt's TikTok account experienced substantial growth, nearly doubling his followers from approximately 3 million to 5.8 million during the campaign period.
- Content Engagement: The sponsored videos collectively amassed over 300 million views, with the hashtag #CucumberSalad surpassed 1.3 billion views on TikTok.

By strategically partnering with a Creator who authentically represented a viral trend, DoorDash effectively demonstrated its commitment to simplicity and ease of use. This case exemplifies the power of aligning brand messaging with organic content to engage target audiences meaningfully.

TikTok Creator Portal: Finding content, communities and creators

The Creator Community and the Role of Brands

The explosive growth of the creator economy has fundamentally changed how value is created, shared, and consumed. As creators redefine influence and reshape industries, brands must ask themselves a critical question: *What role do we play in this new ecosystem?*

Creators—once seen as individuals chasing virality—are now operating as full-scale enterprises. In many cases, they command more attention, loyalty, and purchasing power than traditional companies. According to Yahoo, the Kardashian empire alone is valued at $1.4 billion—a testament to how trust has shifted from institutions to individuals.

This shift has created a new power dynamic. Direct-to-consumer relationships, once the domain of big brands, are now owned by creators who engage audiences with authenticity, storytelling, and community-first thinking. The result? Brands are no longer the gatekeepers of culture—they're guests.

The Evolution of Influence

The creator economy is no longer a niche market—it's a global force. Currently valued at $191.5 billion, it's projected to exceed $525 billion by 2030, growing at a 22.5% compound annual growth rate[48]. Another estimate by Goldman Sachs suggests it could approach $480 billion by 2027 as monetization platforms mature and creator-led businesses scale globally.

This rapid expansion is fueled by platforms like TikTok, YouTube, Shopify, and Etsy—tools that empower individuals to build personal brands, launch products, and connect with audiences directly. With seamless monetization, frictionless global distribution, and community-driven content models, creators now operate with the reach and influence of legacy brands.

Investors are taking notice. From fashion designers and fitness coaches to niche TikTokers and YouTubers, creators are attracting significant funding to expand their product offerings, diversify their content, and enter new markets.

The takeaway? Creators are curating culture and commanding commerce. And in a landscape where people follow *people*, traditional brands need to rethink how they earn attention—and trust.

The Role of Brands in the Creator Era

The last few years have forced a reckoning. As we moved through global disruptions, social shifts, and a growing demand for transparency, consumers became more values-driven, more selective, and more connected—yet also more isolated and overwhelmed.

This is where brands have a renewed opportunity.

Leading companies are beginning to understand that loyalty is no longer about product quality or convenience alone. It's about shared values, cultural relevance, and emotional connection. People don't want to be sold to—they want to be seen. They want to feel something.

---

[48] https://explodingtopics.com/blog/creator-economy-market-size

Today, successful brands are embedding themselves into communities instead of expecting communities to come to them. They're adopting a more human, localized, and relational approach—one that puts purpose before promotion and people before products.

It's not about being *at* a city anymore. It's about being *of* it.

From Status to Kinship:
The Rise of Meaningful Connection

We're witnessing a shift from status-based consumption to values-based belonging. Community is no longer just a marketing strategy—it's a growth engine. To succeed in this space, brands must embrace a kinship mindset: fostering real, two-way relationships built on authenticity, shared passions, and cultural participation.

Spotify offers a masterclass in this approach. Its annual "Spotify Wrapped" campaign turns listener data into deeply personal storytelling—creating shareable, emotional moments for millions. Users celebrate their top songs, rediscover artists, and feel seen by a brand that doesn't just serve them—but *knows* them. This level of personalization builds lasting loyalty and keeps both users and creators engaged. The takeaway for brands? Stop interrupting. Start integrating.

Spotify even curates a personalized 'Top Songs of the Year' playlist, reflecting your listening habits and recommending new artists and tracks—bringing a human, personal touch that feels impossible not to love.

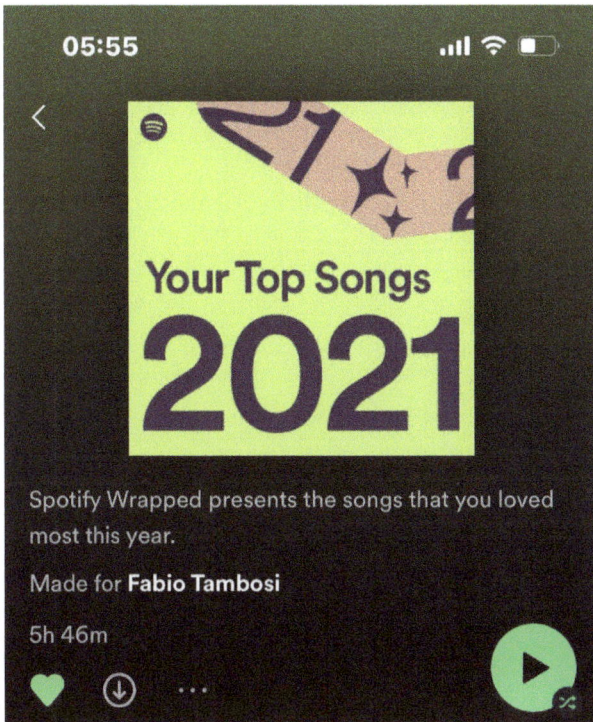

Technology as a Bridge, Not a Barrier

Platforms like Shopify, Stripe, Etsy, and Adyen have democratized access to global markets. Creators and brands alike can now serve customers anywhere, anytime—with personalized products and seamless experiences. Spotify, for instance, uses listener data not just to recommend songs, but to strengthen its community and promote emerging artists.

This is the future: personalized, data-informed, and community-driven.

Instead of sending mass discounts, brands should use digital tools to create experiences that feel personal, timely, and relevant. The goal is no longer just conversion—it's *connection*.

The Call to Brands:
Bring Value, Not Just Visibility

The path forward is clear. Brands must move beyond transactions and start building trust. They must shift from mass communication to meaningful participation. Consumers don't want to be targeted—they want to be understood.

In a world defined by creators, community, and culture, brands have a choice: remain observers or become active participants.

By embracing a more human approach—one rooted in authenticity, purpose, and personalization—brands can build not only awareness but belonging. And in today's world, that's the most powerful currency there is.

Beyond the Screen:
New Ways to Build and Activate Fandom

Social media has revolutionized fandom culture, making once-niche communities global, accessible, and more influential than ever. In the past, being a fan of a lesser-known artist, TV show, or game often meant limited connections. Today, that same fan can instantly find— or build—a thriving community of like-minded people across the world.

For brands, this shift presents a massive opportunity. But simply inserting yourself into a fandom isn't enough—you need to earn your place by understanding the culture, engaging authentically, and adding real value.

So, how can brands successfully integrate into these passionate communities? Let's break it down[49]. According to Instagram's 2024 Trend Talk, some of the most engaged and fastest-growing fandoms on social media right now include:

TV Series & Streaming Platforms

TV shows and streaming platforms are finding new ways to grow dedicated fan bases. By treating their talent like influencers, they're crafting authentic mini-stories and social-only

---

[49] https://www.dashsocial.com/blog/fandom-culture

plotlines that keep viewers not just engaged but fully immersed. A prime example? ABC's *Dancing with the Stars* is absolutely nailing this approach.

Over the past year, the show has seen a surge in younger viewers tuning in and actively voting for their favorite contestants each week. A lot of this success comes down to TikTok. Younger audiences are connecting with the show's talent—both professional dancers and celebrities—on a deeper level, driving real-time engagement.

Now in its 33rd season, the show has had its fair share of viral moments. Think Witney Carson and Danny Amendola's iconic leg lift that everyone tried to recreate, Ilona Maher's relatable *"Not too well, Carrie Ann"* quip, or the drama-filled "romance" between Brooks Nader and Gleb Savchenko that kept fans buzzing on social media long after the duo was eliminated. Gen Z's love for TikTok has breathed new life into the show, expanding its fandom like never before.

As the creator economy evolves and social media content adapts to ever-changing consumer demands, brands and entertainment platforms must seize the moment. TikTok, YouTube, Spotify, and other platforms offer incredible opportunities to connect with fans.

By creating relatable, relevant content with authentic partners and staying on top of trends, brands can build an army of fans eager to champion their message and amplify their reach.

The Timeless Power of TV Fandoms

Television has always had a unique ability to create lasting emotional connections. Unlike a one-time viral moment or a trending topic that fades, great TV shows build deep, enduring fandoms that can span decades. Whether it's the subject matter, the characters, or the actors who bring them to life, the most iconic shows don't just entertain—they inspire devotion.

Some fandoms never fade. *Sex and the City* aired its finale in 2004, yet nearly 20 years later, TikTok is flooded with fashion influencers searching for the perfect "Carrie Bradshaw dress," while other creators passionately debate *Big vs. Aiden* as if the series just wrapped last week.

The digital era has amplified TV fandoms like never before. Social media platforms have become virtual playgrounds for fans to relive iconic moments, analyze character arcs, and create new cultural conversations. Shows that ended years ago continue to thrive because their communities keep them alive through memes, discussions, and nostalgia-driven content.

Here are some of the most enduring TV show fandoms that dominate social media:

- *Friends* – From Ross's "pivot" scene to the never-ending debate about whether they were "on a break," *Friends* is a cultural touchstone that continues to dominate memes, GIFs, and fan discussions.

- *Breaking Bad* – Years after its finale, theories, Easter eggs, and character analyses still trend online, proving that Walter White's legacy is far from over.

- *Stranger Things* – A modern phenomenon, this show's blend of nostalgia, horror, and coming-of-age storytelling has fueled one of the most passionate online fanbases.

- *Supernatural* – A show that ran for 15 seasons and still maintains an active fandom through conventions, social content, and dedicated fan fiction.

- *Game of Thrones* – Despite a divisive final season, this show's fandom remains strong, with spin-offs, theories, and character deep dives still driving conversations.

What makes these shows stand the test of time? It's not just great storytelling—it's the ability to create a world where fans feel invested and emotionally connected. They don't just watch; they participate, discuss, debate, and keep the story alive long after the credits roll.

For brand leaders, the lesson here is clear: fandom isn't built in a single moment—it's nurtured through engagement, community, and giving people something they truly care about.

The Creator Community and the Monetization of Influence

How to Turn Influence Into Business Value

We're living in the era of digital influence—where creators aren't just personalities, they're platforms. The creator economy has shifted power from traditional media to individuals who build trust, shape culture, and move markets.

Influencer marketing is no longer optional. It's a proven, scalable business lever that enables brands to build emotional connection, increase retention, and drive sustainable growth. In this section, I'll show you how creators like Mr. Beast, Kim Kardashian, Charlie D'Amelio and many others have changed the game—and how you can use Influencer Relationship Management (IRM) to do the same.

From Creative Control to Creative Collaboration

The most successful influencer strategies are rooted in co-creation. When you match the right voice with the right message at the right moment, you create content that aligns with consumer intent—not just brand goals. That's when influence becomes impact.

Today, people trust people—not logos. Kim Kardashian, with over 357 million[50] Instagram followers, commands more daily engagement than most Fortune 100 brands. That's not just vanity metrics. That's influence at scale.

As Kim said on The BoF Podcast[51]:

> *"An influencer really relates to an everyday person and inspires them."*

And that's the shift. Creators are now storytellers, producers, and distributors—many with more cultural reach than legacy media channels.

The New Media Model

Social media hasn't just disrupted television—it's replaced it. Creators are now the bridge between culture and commerce, delivering real-time content that's raw, relatable, and real. Platforms like Instagram give them the tools to build and monetize engaged audiences—something brands can tap into with the right approach.

Take Instagram Stories and Live, for example. Branded content typically sees an engagement rate of 3%. Influencers like Kim Kardashian average 9%. Why the difference? Because people crave authenticity—and they're tuning in to *people*, not polished brand messages.

Brands that win in this space are the ones that partner with creators who share their values, not just their reach. The goal isn't a one-time post—it's a journey built on shared purpose.

It's Not Sponsorship—It's Strategy

When done right, influencer marketing is one of the most cost-effective and high-impact strategies available to modern brands. It's a retention tool. A growth engine. A shortcut to relevance.

The numbers speak for themselves:

* The Top 10 global creators and influencers collectively reach *1.4 billion followers*[52].

---

[50] https://www.instagram.com/kimkardashian/?hl=en

[51] https://www.youtube.com/watch?v=ZeKO7LQ_tjw

[52] https://www.forbes.com/sites/stevenbertoni/2024/10/28/top-creators-2024-the-influencers-turning-buzz-into-billions/

- If you identify the right passion points, micro-moments, and aligned voices, your message doesn't just travel—it multiplies.

And this isn't theory. Let's look at the economics.

The Influencer ROI Model: A Kim Kardashian Example

Let's assume Kim posts an Instagram Story to her 357 million followers. With a 9% engagement rate, that's *32.1 million engagements* per story.

Using a conservative *3% conversion rate* (a standard e-commerce benchmark), her post could drive *963,000 direct-to-consumer purchases*.

Now factor in retention. Industry data shows it costs *5x more to acquire a new customer* than to retain an existing one. If the average acquisition cost is *$55 and retention cost is $11*, that's a *$44 savings per retained buyer*.

Let's say Kim helps *retain 80% of those buyers*—comparable to brands like Apple or Amazon. That's *770,400 retained buying customers*.

Now multiply that by the *$44 in savings*.

That's *$33.9 million* in marketing value generated by one influencer, through one channel, with one strategic partnership.

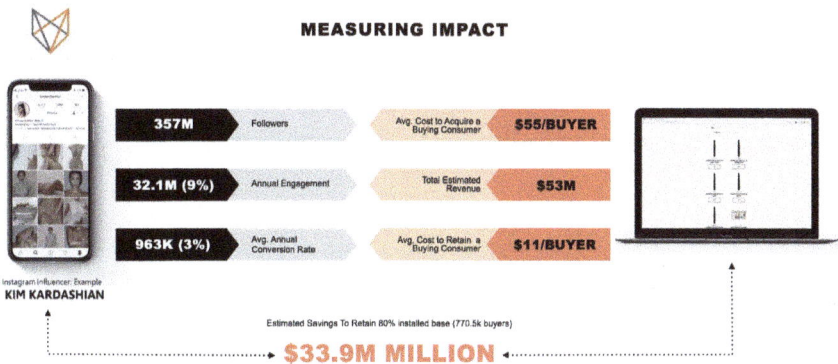

MEASURING IMPACT

357M	Followers	Avg. Cost to Acquire a Buying Consumer	$55/BUYER
32.1M (9%)	Annual Engagement	Total Estimated Revenue	$53M
963K (3%)	Avg. Annual Conversion Rate	Avg. Cost to Retain a Buying Consumer	$11/BUYER

Instagram Influencer: Example
KIM KARDASHIAN

Estimated Savings To Retain 80% installed base (770.5k buyers)

$33.9M MILLION

The Bottom Line: Influence Is a Business Lever

This isn't about celebrity. It's about alignment, intention, and strategy.

Influencers are modern media networks. When you work with them authentically, you don't just cut through the noise—you create value. Value for your brand. Value for your consumers. And value for your bottom line.

Now is the time to rethink your marketing mix. Build influencer relationships that go beyond vanity metrics. Invest in creators who align with your purpose. And most importantly, measure success not just by reach—but by retention, relevance, and real impact.

Influence is currency. Use it wisely.

Brands Tapping Into Fandom Culture: Kosas x Bridgerton[53]

Kosas, a beauty brand known for its "makeup for skincare freaks" positioning, has mastered the art of blending fandom culture with social media marketing. The brand consistently stays ahead by leveraging viral TikTok trends, popular sounds, and cultural moments to engage its audience authentically.

Image credit: @kosas

A standout example? Kosas seamlessly tied its new baked blush collection to the excitement surrounding Netflix's hit series *Bridgerton*. By matching characters from the show with specific blush shades, the brand created an organic, conversation-driving campaign that resonated with both beauty lovers and *Bridgerton* fans alike.

This approach not only capitalized on the buzz around *Bridgerton's* third season but also made the product launch feel like an extension of the fandom—encouraging users to engage, share, and purchase the blush that matched their favorite character.

---

[53] https://www.dashsocial.com/blog/fandom-culture

The Power of Gaming Fandoms

Gaming isn't just a pastime—it's a culture. Video game fandoms are some of the most passionate, engaged, and community-driven in the world. Unlike traditional entertainment, where engagement ends when the credits roll, gaming offers continuous interaction, evolving storylines, and multiplayer experiences that turn players into lifelong fans.

Image credit: @londonlaz

What makes gaming fandoms so strong?

1. Game-Specific Lore & World-Building – Many video games create expansive universes with deep lore, giving players endless content to explore, dissect, and discuss. Whether it's uncovering Easter eggs in *Zelda* or diving into the complex narratives of *Five Nights at Freddy's*, fans love theories, storytelling, and speculation.

2. Always-On Engagement – Gaming content never stops. With live-streaming platforms like Twitch and YouTube Gaming, players and creators share gameplay, strategies, and reactions 24/7, keeping the conversation alive and the hype growing.

3. Constant Content Supply – Unlike movies or TV shows that have long breaks between seasons, the gaming world is always moving. Whether it's updates, DLCs, esports competitions, or fan-created mods, there's always something new to play, watch, and talk about.

Some of the biggest gaming fandoms that dominate social media today include:

- Minecraft – A creative sandbox game with infinite possibilities, spawning countless YouTube channels, TikTok tutorials, and fan-made worlds.

- Grand Theft Auto – Rockstar Games has mastered the art of building hype, and even years after release, *GTA* communities are buzzing with mods, updates, and leaks for the next installment.

- Five Nights at Freddy's (FNAF) – A horror game with rich lore, fan theories, and a recent movie adaptation that reignited its fandom across multiple platforms.

- Fortnite – More than just a battle royale, *Fortnite* is a cultural phenomenon, blending gaming, music, and pop culture crossovers with Marvel, Star Wars, and even real-world concerts.

- Zelda – With *Tears of the Kingdom* breathing new life into the *Zelda* franchise, fans continue to celebrate, create, and uncover hidden secrets in one of the most iconic gaming series of all time.

One of the best examples of gaming fandom in action? The rise of *Fortnite*'s viral moments. Creator Landon, for instance, used the now-famous *Fortnite* song in a video where he played *Fortnite* inside his Tesla. The twist? Landon isn't even primarily a gaming content creator. This crossover moment worked because it seamlessly blended pop culture with gaming, proving that *Fortnite*'s influence extends beyond its player base—it's an internet phenomenon.

For brands, gaming isn't just about the games themselves—it's about tapping into the culture, language, and communities that make these fandoms thrive. Whether you're collaborating with streamers, launching interactive campaigns, or engaging in the conversation, gaming fandoms offer an unparalleled opportunity to connect, create, and build lasting relationships.

Counter-Strike 2:
Two Decades of Fandom, Powered by EFG

Since 2000, *Counter-Strike* has been more than just a game—it's been a culture, a competitive battleground, and a global community that has shaped the modern esports landscape. At the heart of this ecosystem is ESL FACEIT Group (EFG), which has played a pivotal role in turning *Counter-Strike* into one of the most engaged gaming communities in the world.

When *Counter-Strike 2* (CS2) was announced, it wasn't just an update—it was a defining moment for millions of fans. Valve's revolutionary upgrade of the frames per second (a.k.a.: FPS), resulting in improvement of the player experience was met with immediate hype, but the game's long-term success was always going to depend on the strength of its competitive scene and community-driven engagement. That's where EFG's legacy of fostering elite competition and grassroots gaming infrastructure became the ultimate accelerant.

How EFG Turned Counter-Strike into a Cultural Phenomenon

- Esports-Driven Growth: Through ESL Pro Tour (EPT), Intel® Extreme Masters (IEM), and FACEIT competitive circuits, EFG has continuously provided a stage for the best players in the world. These tournaments don't just bring millions of viewers—they create legendary rivalries, iconic plays, and unforgettable moments that fuel engagement and fan devotion. In 2024 alone, IEM broadcasts drew 162 million hours watched and nearly 160,000 attendees[54].

- Community-Powered Engagement: FACEIT, the leading competitive gaming platform, has provided *Counter-Strike* players with a robust, structured matchmaking system for years, bridging the gap between casual and pro-level play. The platform's ranking system, custom leagues, and anti-cheat technology have made it the go-to place for serious *CS2* players.

- Creator & Influencer-Backed Growth: Through its partnerships with top streamers, analysts, and esports pros, EFG has amplified *Counter-Strike's* presence across Twitch, YouTube, and TikTok, ensuring that the game's content ecosystem remains dynamic and ever-growing.

- A Competitive Ecosystem That Fuels the Game: Unlike other games that rely on updates and patches to keep players engaged, *Counter-Strike's* fanbase thrives on the competitive ecosystem that EFG has nurtured. Events like IEM Cologne, ESL Challenger, and the FACEIT Major are more than just tournaments—they're cultural milestones in the *CS* calendar that drive conversation, engagement, and community investment.

The Launch of CS2:
A Great Example of Community-First Marketing

When Valve released *Counter-Strike 2*, they didn't flood the market with traditional advertising. Instead, they leaned into the strength of the community, empowering platforms like FACEIT and ESL tournaments to organically showcase the game's innovations.

---

[54] https://venturebeat.com/gaming-business/esl-faceit-group-and-intel-renew-multi-year-esports-partnership-on-counter-strike/

By letting the major players in the industry seamlessly adopt the new game, Valve allowed the gaming community to experience the introduction of their new version in an organic and authentic way rather than have it pushed at them via traditional marketing campaigns.

The Takeaway: The Power of a Thriving Ecosystem

Counter-Strike 2 isn't just surviving—it's thriving, in large part because of the 20-year foundation of community-driven engagement built by ESL FACEIT Group. The lesson for brands is clear: Fandom isn't built overnight. It takes authentic engagement, competitive infrastructure, and a deep understanding of what keeps players invested.

For any game or brand looking to build lasting engagement, the blueprint is simple: Create a space where fans can compete, create, and connect—and then let the community take it from there.

Florence by Mills x Billie Eilish: Fandom in Action

Florence by Mills, the beauty brand founded by Millie Bobby Brown, has effectively harnessed fandom culture in its social media marketing strategies. In a notable TikTok campaign, the brand utilized lyrics from Billie Eilish's trending song *"Birds of a Feather,"* calling out its products as items consumers would "love until the day [they] die." This approach not only capitalized on the song's popularity but also resonated with Billie Eilish's extensive fanbase, thereby increasing the content's visibility and engagement.

Image credit: @florencebymills

The rationale behind this strategy is supported by data highlighting the impact of music trends on social media engagement. According to a report by The Guardian, older songs have been experiencing a resurgence on platforms like TikTok, with 19 of the top 50 TikTok tracks in the UK in 2024 being more than five years old. This trend indicates that leveraging popular music, regardless of its release date, can significantly enhance content reach and audience interaction[55].

---

[55] https://www.theguardian.com/technology/2024/dec/25/older-music-has-been-getting-a-second-life-on-tiktok-data-shows

By aligning their products with a viral song, Florence by Mills effectively tapped into existing fan communities, creating content that was both relatable and shareable. This strategy not only increased brand awareness but also fostered a deeper connection with a diverse audience, demonstrating the power of integrating fandom culture into social media marketing.

The Rise of Athlete-Led Social Media Fandom

In today's digital world, the way fans connect with athletes has completely transformed. It used to be simple: you admired an athlete for their performance on the field, court, or track. Over time, that admiration might have grown into a personal connection, fueled by post-game interviews, magazine features, or the occasional documentary.

It was a one-way street—athletes played, and fans watched.

Now? Social media has rewritten the rules. Today, athletes are active storytellers, content creators, and owners of their personal brands. They engage directly with fans in real-time, shaping narratives beyond the game. This shift has turned individual athletes into powerful fandom engines, bringing new audiences into sports in ways that were never possible before.

In today's digital landscape, social media has revolutionized the way fans connect with athletes, transforming passive spectators into engaged communities. This shift has redefined sports fandom, making it more personal and accessible than ever.

Expanding Reach, Building Loyalty

The expanse social presence of athletes introduces new audiences to sports, turning casual viewers into passionate fans. For brands and teams, investing in athlete-driven social engagement isn't just smart—it's essential for sustained growth and deeper fan loyalty.

From Social Media to Stadiums: The New Fan Journey

Traditionally, fans discovered athletes through live games or televised events, with personal insights limited to post-game interviews or occasional media features. Now, platforms like TikTok, Instagram, and YouTube allow fans to engage with athletes' personalities, values, and daily lives directly. This personal connection often precedes any on-field performance, attracting even non-sports enthusiasts to follow and support athletes and their teams.

Case in Point: Jared McCain

Before making his mark at Duke University and with the Philadelphia 76ers, Jared McCain built a substantial following on TikTok. His blend of basketball highlights and relatable content amassed over 2 million followers, many of whom were not traditional basketball fans. This online presence translated into increased viewership and support during his games, exemplifying how social media can broaden an athlete's fan base.

The Cristiano Ronaldo Phenomenon

Cristiano Ronaldo stands as a testament to the power of social media in building a global fan community. As of September 2024, Ronaldo became the first individual to surpass 1 billion followers across platforms, including 638 million on Instagram, 170 million on Facebook, and 113 million on X (formerly Twitter). This unparalleled reach allows him to engage with fans worldwide, transcending geographic and cultural barriers[56].

Ronaldo's social media strategy offers fans a window into his life beyond the pitch, sharing personal milestones, training routines, and philanthropic efforts. This transparency fosters a deep sense of community and loyalty among his followers. Moreover, his collaborations with popular content creators, such as YouTube sensation MrBeast, have expanded his audience further. A recent video featuring the duo garnered over 1 million views within 30 minutes of its release[57], highlighting the synergistic potential of such partnerships.

Implications for Teams and Leagues

The rise of athlete-driven social media influence offers significant benefits to sports teams and leagues. Athletes' personal brands can attract new fans, increase merchandise sales, and boost game viewership. By encouraging and supporting players in their social media endeavors, organizations can tap into these expansive networks, fostering a more engaged and diverse fan base.

Social media has become an indispensable tool in modern sports fandom. Athletes who authentically share their lives and values can build robust, loyal communities that enhance both their personal brand and the broader appeal of their sport.

---

[56] https://www.espn.com/soccer/story/_/id/41241628/cristiano-ronaldo-celebrates-one-billion-social-media-followers

[57] https://talksport.com/football/2304731/cristiano-ronaldo-breaks-the-internet-mr-beast/

Social Media as a Fandom Accelerator:
The Caitlin Clark Effect

A cultural phenomenon doesn't need to *start* on social media to *thrive* on it—but social can rapidly accelerate visibility, scale connection, and convert admiration into true fandom. Caitlin Clark's rise is a masterclass in this dynamic.

While her game-changing presence on the basketball court ignited attention, it was social media that transformed her into a cultural icon. Her electrifying performances, swagger, and authenticity were sliced into viral clips, shared across TikTok, X, and Instagram—turning every three-pointer and behind-the-back assist into a moment of mass connection. Fans didn't just watch; they engaged, remixed, reacted, and rallied.

This amplification had tangible results. WNBA attendance in 2024 jumped by 48%, with over 2.35 million fans packing arenas—a 20-year high. Her debut game smashed viewership records, while her mere presence boosted the local Indianapolis economy by $36.5 million and contributed over 25% of the WNBA's total revenue.

Clark didn't build her fandom through ads or press releases. She did it through moments. And social media turned those moments into movements—connecting people not just to her skills, but to her story.

The takeaway? Social media isn't just a channel for reach. When used intentionally, it becomes a connection engine—one that can turn talent into influence, and influence into cultural relevance.

Fandom Is Big Business:
How Caitlin Clark Turned Attention Into Revenue

The Caitlin Clark Effect serves as a powerful example of how social media can transform talent into cultural capital—and cultural capital into economic value. Her rise didn't originate on social platforms, but they became the engine that scaled her impact, fueled fan engagement, and catalyzed real business outcomes.

From boosting WNBA attendance and viewership to attracting major sponsorship dollars and reshaping perceptions of women's sports, her story is a blueprint for brand building in the digital age.

Five key learnings emerge:

1. Authentic talent becomes magnetic when amplified through social media,
2. Viral moments drive emotional connection, which drives loyalty,
3. Cultural relevance unlocks commercial value,
4. Social media can democratize exposure—giving women's sports a louder voice and bigger platform,
5. A well-timed digital strategy can turn a rising star into an industry-wide movement. Caitlin's journey reminds us that connection is the currency—and social is the marketplace.

Caitlin Clark's ascent proves that in today's attention economy, fandom isn't just a byproduct of success—it's a business strategy. For brands, leagues, and leaders looking to break through the noise, the lesson is clear: invest in storytelling, lean into culture, and use social media not just to be seen, but to be felt. When connection becomes your KPI, growth follows.

Turning Fandom Into A Growth Driver

Social media has become one of the most powerful tools for brand growth, and fandom sits at the heart of that success. A strong, engaged community isn't just about likes and shares—it translates directly into real business impact.

For teams, leagues, and universities, investing in their athletes' personal brands is a game-changer. When athletes build authentic connections with fans, it fuels deeper loyalty, higher engagement, and increased viewership. The effect is undeniable: In 2023, college athletes who maximized their social media presence saw their NIL (Name, Image, and Likeness) value increase by an average of 12x, proving that fandom-driven social influence is a direct revenue driver[58].

For brands, partnering with athletes who have an authentic social media presence isn't just about exposure—it's about trust. Nearly 50% of millennials say they are more likely to buy products endorsed by their favorite NFL players[59]. The impact extends beyond men's sports

---

[58] https://biz.opendorse.com/report-commercial-nil-athletes-influencers/#:~:text=As%20influencer%20marketing%20continues%20to,reach%20of%20the%20creator%20economy.

[59] https://www.nilnetwork.com/the-rise-of-social-media-first-sports-fandom/

too—one in three fans holds a more favorable view of brands that sponsor female athletes[60]. These aren't just numbers; they're proof that when brands tap into fandoms the right way, they build credibility, drive conversions, and create long-term consumer loyalty.

As social media continues to redefine how fans connect with sports, entertainment, and culture, brands that invest in building real, meaningful communities will separate themselves from the rest. Winning Brands aren't just selling products—they are igniting passion, fostering loyalty, and creating experiences that fans want to be part of.

From Followers to Fanatics: The Fandom Playbook

Social media isn't just a marketing channel—it's a cultural force. The brands, teams, and athletes that win aren't the ones shouting the loudest; they're the ones building real, emotional connections. Fandom isn't built on ads or algorithms—it's built on moments, conversations, and shared experiences.

So, the real question isn't if you should tap into fandom culture. It's how far you're willing to go to turn passive followers into die-hard believers.

What's next? It's time to move beyond engagement and into unforgettable experiences— because that's where loyalty is born, and winning brands are made.

---

[60] https://www.nielsen.com/insights/2023/womens-sports-viewership-on-the-rise/

CHAPTER 8
DESIGNING DISTINCTION—
HOW EXPERIENCES BUILD BRAND VALUE

In a marketplace where products are easily replicated and attention is fleeting, brand experiences have become one of the most powerful differentiators. Exceptional experiences go beyond utility or design—they spark emotion, create memories, and turn casual buyers into lifelong advocates.

Unforgettable experiences are the foundation of modern fandom. They don't just attract attention; they build emotional capital. These moments create lasting bonds, encourage organic sharing, and deepen connection far beyond the initial transaction.

Why does this matter for business?

- **It drives emotional loyalty.** Customers return to brands that make them feel something. Emotion sustains engagement long after the sale.

- **It makes your brand non-substitutable.** In saturated markets, experience is often the only meaningful differentiator.

- **It fuels organic growth.** The most credible marketing comes from fans who voluntarily share their experiences.

The real question isn't *if* experiences matter—but how you design them intentionally to create impact, scale engagement, and drive long-term brand value.

In this chapter, we'll explore frameworks and examples for creating memorable, brand-defining experiences—and show how they directly contribute to business growth and market leadership.

Connected Fans Drive Bigger Growth

Maintaining open communication channels with your fans is essential for building loyalty and driving revenue growth. Engaged customers are more likely to make repeat purchases and advocate for your brand. For instance, 93% of customers are likely to make repeat purchases with companies that offer excellent customer service[61].

Implementing strategies like personalized interactions and responsive customer service can significantly enhance customer retention. Studies have shown that increasing customer retention rates by just 5% can increase profits by 25% to 95%.

By leveraging automation tools and AI software to promptly address inquiries, while ensuring the availability of human interaction when needed, brands can foster stronger relationships with their audience. This approach not only meets customer expectations but also positions your brand as accessible and customer-centric, leading to increased loyalty and revenue.

Make It Easy to Engage

Opening direct communication with your fans isn't just a courtesy—it's a competitive advantage. Brands that actively engage build stronger trust, which leads to higher retention, increased lifetime value, and ultimately, revenue growth.

Here's how to make it happen:

- Segment & Personalize: Not all fans want the same thing. Use engagement data from your social channels, email lists, and purchase behavior to segment your audience and tailor your interactions.

- Leverage AI Without Losing the Human Touch: Chatbots and AI-driven customer service tools can help you respond instantly, but they should enhance—not replace—human interaction.

- Community-Led Engagement: Encourage fans to engage with each other, creating a self-sustaining loop of discussion and advocacy.

---

[61] https://www.helpscout.com/75-customer-service-facts-quotes-statistics/

Becoming a winning brand isn't just about selling. It's about creating an ongoing conversation that keeps fans invested in your brand, leading to loyalty, advocacy, and long-term revenue growth.

Emotional Engagement:
Tapping into What Moves Your Audience

Fans are driven by emotion, and the brands that understand and harness these emotions build lasting loyalty. To create experiences that truly resonate, you need to know what inspires, excites, and motivates your audience.

How to Make It Happen:

1. Know Your Audience: Conduct surveys, focus groups, and social media listening to uncover their deepest motivations, fears, and desires.
2. Create Meaningful Themes: Align your brand experiences with emotions that matter—nostalgia, joy, empowerment, or belonging.
3. Engage the Senses: Use powerful imagery, music, and storytelling to evoke the right emotional response.

From Transactions to Relationships:
Why Experiences Matter More Than Products

Modern consumers aren't just buying products—they're investing in brands that align with their values and lifestyles. The shift from transactional marketing to emotional engagement is what turns casual buyers into lifelong fans.

Want to build a brand that people don't just buy from, but believe in? Start by delivering unforgettable experiences.

Gen Z: The Experience-First Generation

For Gen Z, experiences matter more than products. Unlike previous generations that equated success with material ownership, Gen Z prioritizes meaning, connection, and shared moments over accumulating things. They aren't chasing bigger houses or flashier cars—they're investing in experiences that enrich their lives and align with their values.

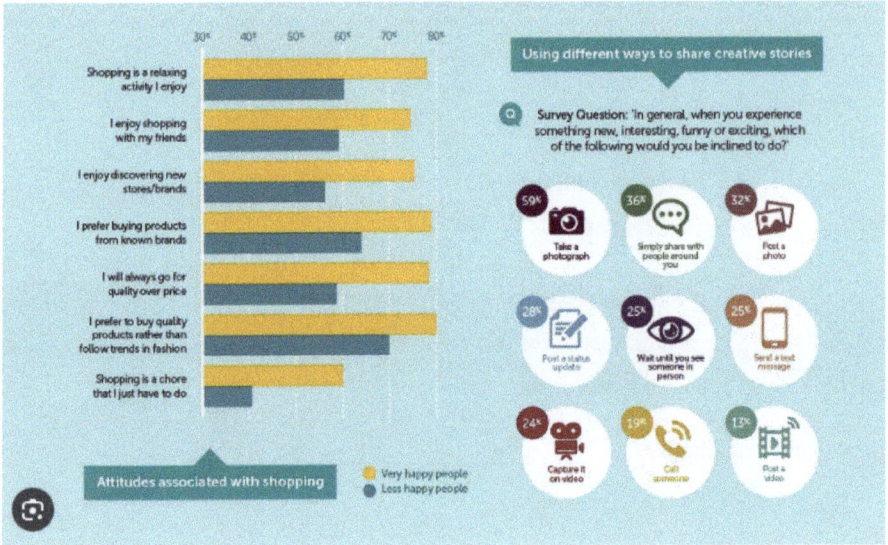

This shift isn't just a passing trend; it's reshaping consumer behavior at its core. Here's why:

They Don't Equate Money with Happiness

Gen Z grew up watching older generations prioritize wealth accumulation—only to see that material success didn't necessarily bring fulfillment. Studies confirm that people report greater happiness after spending money on experiences rather than products. Brands that tap into this insight—offering exclusive events, immersive moments, or interactive storytelling—win their loyalty.

They Avoid Debt & Prioritize Flexibility

Having witnessed financial crises and growing up under the weight of student loan debt (averaging $39,000 per borrower), Gen Z resists unnecessary financial burdens. Many choose "Generation Rent" lifestyles, favoring flexibility over ownership. Instead of saving for a mortgage, they're investing in travel, concerts, and unique digital experiences.

Social Media Fuels the Experience Economy

Gen Z is the first generation to grow up fully immersed in social media. Their digital lives are deeply intertwined with their real ones, and experiences—whether a festival, adventure, or cultural moment—are prime social currency. A new car doesn't generate the same engagement as a bucket-list trip or front-row concert access. Experiences aren't just enjoyed; they're shared, amplifying their value.

They Seek Brands That Offer More Than Just Products

Gen Z is deeply loyal to brands that create meaningful, memorable moments. They don't just want to buy—they want to belong. Companies that integrate experiential elements into their marketing—like exclusive product drops, interactive events, and digital-first storytelling—stand out in an oversaturated marketplace.

This shift has fueled the rise of the **experience economy**, where brands must offer more than just transactions; they must create moments that are unforgettable, shareable, and deeply personal.

Bringing the Experience Economy to Life

Gen Z's preference for experiences over possessions means brands must go beyond selling products—they need to create meaningful interactions. To truly engage this audience, brands should:

Focus on the Journey

Every touchpoint matters. From the first discovery to long-term loyalty, the experience should feel seamless, intentional, and emotionally resonant. Fans don't just buy into a product—they buy into a brand's world.

Incorporate Rituals

Traditions build emotional connections. Whether it's an annual event, exclusive product drops, or interactive fan moments, creating signature experiences gives fans something to anticipate and participate in.

Offer Value Beyond the Product

The most successful brands don't just sell—they educate, entertain, and inspire. By offering content, experiences, and moments that enrich fans' lives, brands transform from being a choice to becoming a lifestyle.

In today's experience-driven economy, brands that embrace these strategies don't just attract customers—they create lifelong fans.

Making Experiences Unforgettable: The Power of Storytelling, Surprise, and Immersion

At the heart of every unforgettable experience is a powerful story. Storytelling isn't just a marketing tactic—it's the foundation of emotional connection. Fans don't just want to buy a product; they want to feel something. And the best way to make them feel? Give them a story they can see themselves in.

Crafting Narratives That Resonate

Stories shape how people relate to your brand. They bring meaning to what you do, turning transactions into relationships and customers into advocates.

Key Ingredients of Impactful Brand Storytelling:

1. Relatable Characters – Whether it's customers, employees, or ambassadors, showcase real people with real emotions. Let fans see themselves in the journey.
2. Conflict and Resolution – Every great story has a challenge to overcome. Show how your brand plays a role in solving problems, inspiring transformation, or making life better.
3. Authenticity – Fans can sniff out inauthenticity from a mile away. Your brand's stories must align with your values and mission—anything less feels forced and forgettable.

And when storytelling is done right, it doesn't just resonate—it drives real impact. Let's take a look at how we put this into action at Saucony, transforming a brand narrative into a movement that fueled both connection and growth.

Inviting Fans Into Your Story: The Power of Shared Journeys

A fan's journey is more than a series of interactions; it's a transformative experience where your brand becomes a catalyst for personal achievement. By understanding and guiding this journey, you can turn casual observers into passionate advocates.

Understanding the Fan's Journey

Fans often begin their relationship with a brand through various touchpoints: a social media post, a friend's recommendation, or an initial purchase. Recognizing these entry points and the subsequent path they take is crucial. By mapping out this journey, you can tailor experiences that resonate at each stage, fostering deeper connections.

Case Study: Saucony's "Call Us Runners" Campaign

At Saucony, our core audience comprised dedicated runners participating in multiple marathons annually. To expand our reach without alienating this base, we conducted in-depth behavioral and psychographic research. This led to the discovery of a subculture: individuals who run regularly but hesitate to label themselves as "runners" due to societal pressures and stereotypes.

In response, we launched the "Call Us Runners" campaign, celebrating the diverse identities of runners:

- Jared Ward, an Olympic athlete, shared: "Some people call me a runner. Others call me a professor. My favorite people call me dad." This highlighted the multifaceted lives of even elite runners.
- Trinidad James, a musician, showcased that running transcends traditional boundaries.
- Jay Ell Alexander, founder of Black Girls RUN!, emphasized running as a tool for community building and personal growth.

This inclusive approach resonated widely, leading to a 6% increase in revenue in 2022, with total sales reaching $505 million.

The Lesson: Fandom Is Built on Emotional Connection[62].

Fans don't just want a product; they want to see themselves in your story. When a brand truly understands its values, mission, and what it can do for fans, it transcends marketing—it becomes part of their lives.

- Meet Fans Where They Are: Understand their motivations and barriers.
- Authentic Storytelling: Share real stories that reflect your audience's experiences.
- Inclusive Messaging: Embrace and celebrate diversity within your community.

---

[62] https://www.business.com/articles/experience-over-goods-the-millennial-shift-in-spending/

By inviting fans on a journey that acknowledges and supports their personal narratives, brands can foster lasting loyalty and drive growth.

And that's the key: meet your fans where they are. On their terms. In their world. The brands that do this don't just attract fans—they create lifelong advocates.

Adding the Unexpected: Surprise and Delight

The most memorable brand experiences often come from the unexpected. When fans feel like they're getting something special, they form a deeper emotional bond with your brand.

Ways to Surprise and Delight Your Fans:

- Unexpected Rewards – Random discounts, free upgrades, or exclusive perks show appreciation and create positive buzz.

- Thoughtful Gestures – A handwritten note, a personalized video message, or early access to a product can turn a customer into a lifelong fan.

- Gamified Surprises – Hide digital Easter eggs, create interactive social challenges, or launch mystery giveaways to keep fans engaged and excited.

Immersive Experiences: Turning Fans into Participants

The strongest connections happen when fans don't just observe but actively participate in your brand's world. Creating immersive experiences gives them a reason to engage and stay invested.

Bringing Your Brand to Life:

- Augmented Reality (AR) – Let fans interact with your brand in new ways, from virtual product try-ons to immersive storytelling campaigns.

- Live Events & Pop-Ups – Give fans a hands-on experience, whether it's through workshops, performances, or behind-the-scenes moments.

- Experiential Campaigns – Create brand experiences that transport fans into your universe, whether it's a fully interactive digital space or a real-world activation.

The brands that master storytelling, surprise, and immersion don't just capture attention—they create movements. They go beyond selling products and instead build emotional connections that stand the test of time. How will you make your brand unforgettable?

Personalization: Connecting Fans as Individuals

Fans don't just want to be part of a crowd—they want to feel seen, valued, and understood for who they are. As people, not just as a part of a group.

Using Data and AI to Deliver Hyper-Personalized Fan Experiences[63]

The biggest challenge brands face today isn't just capturing attention—it's maintaining relevance. That's where personalization comes in. In a world where nearly *70% of consumers* are more likely to buy from brands that offer personalized experiences, failing to deliver means leaving revenue and loyalty on the table.

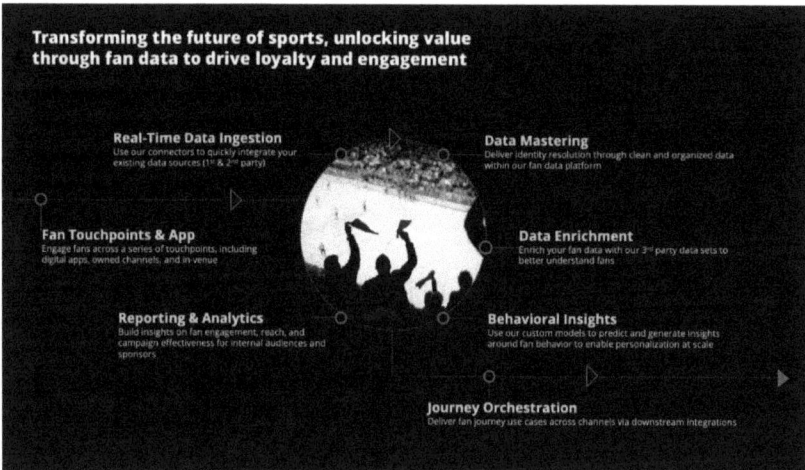

Transforming the future of sports, unlocking value through fan data to drive loyalty and engagement

Real-Time Data Ingestion
Use our connectors to quickly integrate your existing data sources (1st & 2nd party)

Data Mastering
Deliver identity resolution through clean and organized data within our fan data platform

Fan Touchpoints & App
Engage fans across a series of touchpoints, including digital apps, owned channels, and in-venue

Data Enrichment
Enrich your fan data with our 3rd party data sets to better understand fans

Reporting & Analytics
Build insights on fan engagement, reach, and campaign effectiveness for internal audiences and sponsors

Behavioral Insights
Use our custom models to predict and generate insights around fan behavior to enable personalization at scale

Journey Orchestration
Deliver fan journey use cases across channels via downstream integrations

By leveraging AI, digital transformation, and deep fan data, brands can create experiences that don't just engage fans but keep them coming back. Thanks to the rapid adoption of AI, personalization at scale is no longer a luxury—it's an expectation.

Tactics to Personalize at Scale

1. Customized Products – Give fans the power to personalize merchandise, from jerseys with their names to exclusive product drops based on their preferences.

---

[63] https://www2.deloitte.com/us/en/pages/consulting/articles/personalized-fan-engagement.html

2.   Tailored Communication – Use behavioral insights to send hyper-relevant content, recommendations, and offers that make every message feel like it was made just for them.

3.   VIP Access & Experiences – Reward loyalty with exclusive behind-the-scenes content, early product releases, or one-on-one interactions with brand ambassadors and athletes.

The Business Case for Personalization

The ROI of personalization is clear. Brands that invest in data-driven personalization see increased engagement, stronger relationships with fans, and higher revenue growth. Sports teams, for example, are leveraging fan data to create curated messaging as a way to *boost ticket sales, drive sponsorship value, and enhance media relationships*—all while delivering more meaningful connections.

The future of fandom isn't about marketing *to* your audience—it's about marketing *with* them, on their terms. And personalization is key to making that happen. How will you make your fans feel like they are truly seen?

Why It Matters:
Turning Engagement Into Lasting Impact

When fans feel seen and valued, they don't just engage—they advocate. Personalization fuels this sense of belonging, but social sharing takes it a step further, turning individual experiences into viral moments that amplify your brand's reach and relevance.

By designing experiences that fans want to share, you're not only deepening their connection but also unlocking organic growth. The future of fandom isn't just about marketing to your audience—it's about creating experiences they can't wait to share. How will you turn engagement into momentum?

Building a Thriving Community:
From Connection to Commitment[64]

Creating a strong brand community isn't just about attracting fans—it's about keeping them engaged in meaningful ways. Social media offers a space for interaction, but with endless distractions, it's easy for your message to get lost. That's why curating a more intentional, fan-led environment is crucial.

Consider creating a dedicated space—whether it's a private app, a membership platform, or a branded forum—where your most loyal supporters can connect without interruption. These spaces should encourage participation, foster deeper discussions, and allow fans to take ownership of their community. When fans feel like they have a stake in something exclusive, they're more likely to stay engaged and invite others to join, fueling organic growth.

Beyond engagement, an exclusive community can also drive revenue. Gated content, premium subscriptions, or members-only events add tangible value while strengthening fan loyalty. People are willing to pay for unique experiences that make them feel closer to the brand they love.

Ways to Build Community That Lasts

1. Host Meetups & Events – Bring fans together in real life or virtually to strengthen their sense of belonging.
2. Create Digital Spaces – Build exclusive forums, Facebook Groups, or Discord servers for ongoing conversations.
3. Celebrate Fan Contributions – Highlight fan-generated content, testimonials, and creative works to deepen emotional investment.

A thriving community doesn't happen by chance—it's built with intention. The brands that win aren't just the ones with the most followers; they're the ones that make every fan feel like they truly belong.

---

[64] https://www.fancircles.com/5-ways-to-grow-your-superfan-community/

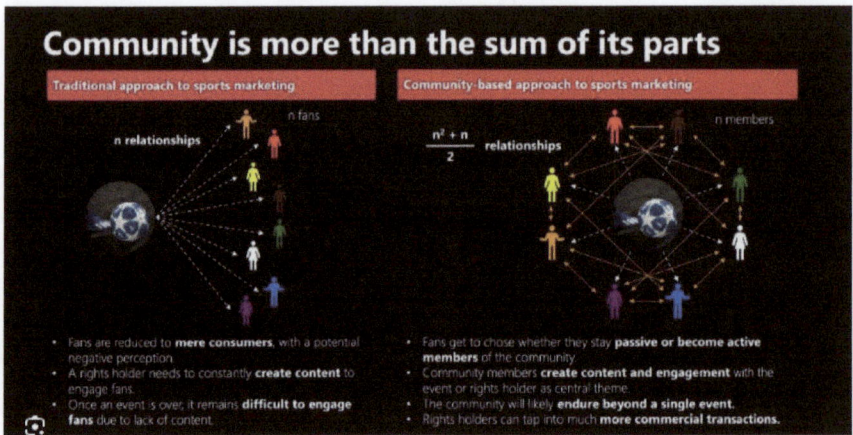

Community is more than the sum of its parts

Traditional approach to sports marketing

n fans

n relationships

Community-based approach to sports marketing

n members

$$\frac{n^2 + n}{2}$$ relationships

- Fans are reduced to **mere consumers**, with a potential negative perception.
- A rights holder needs to constantly **create content** to engage fans.
- Once an event is over, it remains **difficult to engage fans** due to lack of content.

- Fans get to chose whether they stay **passive or become active members** of the community.
- Community members **create content and engagement** with the event or rights holder as central theme.
- The community will likely **endure beyond a single event**.
- Rights holders can tap into much **more commercial transactions**.

Bringing Fans Closer: Transparency & Engagement

Building an unforgettable brand isn't just about what you deliver—it's about how you involve your fans in the journey. The most engaged communities thrive on access, authenticity, and a sense of participation. Here's how you can create deeper emotional connections by making fans feel like insiders.

Show Fans Behind the Scenes

People don't just want to see the finished product—they want to experience the process, the passion, and the people behind it. Offering behind-the-scenes access builds trust and fosters a deeper emotional connection.

1. Live Streaming & BTS Content – Use Instagram Live, TikTok, or YouTube to showcase product development, rehearsals, athlete training sessions, or event preparations in real time.
2. Day-in-the-Life Features – Highlight key figures in your brand, from employees and creators to athletes and executives, giving fans a personal look at the faces behind the brand.
3. Raw & Unfiltered Moments – Share real, unscripted content that humanizes your brand and builds authenticity.

Leverage Fan Feedback to Improve & Innovate

Many brands make the mistake of assuming they know what their fans want—without actually asking them. Direct fan feedback is one of the most valuable tools for refining experiences and strengthening loyalty.

1. Engage Through Polls & Surveys – Use Instagram Stories, Twitter polls, or in-app surveys to let fans voice their opinions on products, content, and brand decisions.
2. Community Listening – Monitor fan conversations across social platforms and forums to identify emerging trends, concerns, and opportunities.
3. Make Fans Part of the Process – Involve fans in product development, campaign ideation, or content creation to make them feel truly invested in your brand's success.

Why It Works

Giving fans insider access and actively listening to their input transforms them from passive consumers into engaged participants. The result? A more passionate, loyal community that not only supports your brand but champions it.

Final Thought:
Experiences Build Winning Brands

The brands that win aren't just the ones with the best products—they're the ones that create moments people *never forget.* Unforgettable experiences fuel emotional connections, drive loyalty, and transform fans into lifelong advocates.

Social media, personalization, and storytelling are powerful tools, but they're only as impactful as the experiences you create with them. When you engage your audience in meaningful ways—when you make them feel something—they won't just buy from you; they'll believe in you

The question isn't whether experiences matter. The question is: How will you make yours unforgettable?

CHAPTER 9
SHAPING CULTURE:
THE TRANSFORMATIONAL POWER OF
INTERACTIVE EXPERIENCES

"In-person experiences drive more lasting brand impressions, with 70% of consumers saying live events help them better understand and remember a brand."
— *Statista & EMI Global Research, 2023*

If the past few years have taught us anything, it's this: digital alone isn't enough. During the COVID-19 pandemic, brands around the world leaned heavily on virtual touchpoints. But in that absence, one truth became undeniable—nothing replaces the power of a live experience.

Live events deliver something digital can't: energy, immersion, and connection that ignite all five senses and leave lasting emotional impact. They don't just engage—they transform. For brands, they are one of the most powerful tools to accelerate trust, foster loyalty, and build fandom that lasts.

This isn't a nostalgic return to physical marketing—it's a strategic imperative.

Over my career, leading experiential and cultural activations for brands like Nike, adidas, and Saucony, I've seen firsthand how live experiences create brand moments that stick—not for days, but for years. When done right, they turn audiences into advocates and fans into brand believers.

Why Interactive Experiences Drive Business Impact:

- *Sensory Engagement:* Live activations create multi-sensory moments—something no scroll or swipe can match.

- *Human Connection:* Face-to-face interaction builds emotional trust faster and deeper than any ad campaign.

- *Earned Amplification:* A powerful event generates organic reach as fans share their experience—turning moments into movements.

Industry leaders understand this. Apple transforms product launches into global media moments. Red Bull uses live stunts to embody its fearless identity. Nike activates local communities to build global loyalty. These are not just events—they are expressions of brand belief systems, and they deliver measurable business outcomes.

If your brand has relied solely on digital tactics, you're leaving emotional equity—and long-term value—on the table.

In this chapter, we'll explore how to strategically design live experiences that elevate your brand, activate your community, and turn moments into movements.

Defining Your Event's Purpose: What's the Goal?

A successful brand activation doesn't start with logistics—it starts with **a clear purpose.** What do you want your event to achieve? Every activation should align with broader brand goals and deliver measurable impact.

Here are the core objectives most successful events aim to accomplish:

- Increase Brand Awareness – Live events introduce your brand to new audiences, expanding reach and visibility in an authentic way.

- Deepen Fan Engagement – Exclusive, immersive experiences strengthen emotional connections, turning casual consumers into loyal brand advocates.

- Drive Sales & Conversions – Product launches, pop-up activations, and in-event exclusives can accelerate sales and create demand.

- Build a Community – Events bring like-minded people together, fostering a sense of belonging and strengthening fan loyalty.

When your event has a defined purpose, you can measure success, allocate resources effectively, and ensure every touchpoint delivers real value.

What Exactly is a Fan Activation?

A fan activation is a strategy designed to turn passive fans into active participants—people who not only support your brand but champion it. It's more than just hosting an event; it's about creating immersive experiences that invite fans to engage, contribute, and feel like they're part of something bigger.

Think interactive activities, real-world challenges, social media-driven campaigns, or exclusive behind-the-scenes access—activations bridge the gap between passive consumption and active participation. And when done right? They create lifelong brand advocates.

Now, let's break down exactly how to craft an event experience that moves fans from spectators to superfans.

Jordan Bred:
40 Years of Legacy, Super Bowl Edition[65]

Nike's first-ever Jordan Brand activation at the Super Bowl was more than a marketing play—it was a statement. By honoring the legacy of the Air Jordan 1 High '85 "Bred" during the biggest sporting event in the U.S., Jordan Brand reinforced its cultural relevance while fueling demand and driving sales.

---

[65] https://www.complex.com/sneakers/a/victor-deng/air-jordan-1-high-85-bred-banned-limited-10k-pairs

How Nike Turned Legacy into Momentum

1. Exclusive Early Access to Create Urgency & Demand

Select retailers, including BSTN, provided limited early releases of the Air Jordan 1 High '85 "Bred," rewarding dedicated sneakerheads and generating hype before the official drop. This scarcity-driven strategy heightened demand, ensuring a rapid sell-out upon release.

2. Immersive, Thematic In-Store Activations

Premium boutiques transformed their spaces into "Unbannable" experiences, paying tribute to the sneaker's controversial origins. These activations didn't just showcase the shoe—they reinforced the cultural mythology behind the Bred 1s, fostering brand loyalty and deeper fan engagement.

3. Athlete-Driven Brand Storytelling on the Super Bowl Stage

Philadelphia Eagles quarterback Jalen Hurts, a Jordan Brand athlete, wore a custom player-exclusive Air Jordan 1 cleat during Super Bowl pregame activities. His on-field presence, combined with the brand's first-ever Super Bowl commercial, cemented Jordan Brand's crossover appeal beyond basketball. Following his MVP-caliber performance, the moment resonated deeply with both sneaker culture and mainstream sports fans, expanding the brand's reach.

The Business Impact: A Bold Play in a Competitive Market

At a time when Jordan Brand is working to sustain momentum in a shifting market, this activation blended history, exclusivity, and live experiences to reignite consumer demand. By strategically aligning with sports culture's biggest stage, Nike didn't just celebrate a sneaker—it reasserted Jordan Brand's dominance in the sneaker and lifestyle space.

Lessons in Legacy: Jordan Brand's Playbook for Success

Nike's first-ever Jordan Brand activation at the Super Bowl was a masterclass in blending heritage, exclusivity, and cultural relevance to drive engagement and sales. By leveraging scarcity, immersive storytelling, and athlete-driven brand moments, the activation reinforced Jordan Brand's legacy while expanding its influence beyond basketball.

Key Takeaways for Brand Leaders:

- Cultural Relevance Matters – Tapping into major cultural moments like the Super Bowl amplifies brand impact.

- Exclusivity Drives Demand – Limited early releases and premium activations create urgency and deepen fan loyalty.

- Athlete Storytelling Elevates Reach – Strategic athlete partnerships enhance credibility and connect with broader audiences.

- Live Experiences Leave a Lasting Impact – Beyond digital campaigns, in-person activations forge deeper emotional connections.

By fusing legacy with innovation, Jordan Brand didn't just celebrate a sneaker—it reignited demand, strengthened fan engagement, and proved the enduring power of live experiences in building a Winning Brands.

Immersive and Interactive Experiences: Engaging Fans Through Innovation

In today's dynamic landscape, brands must go beyond traditional marketing to create memorable, immersive experiences that actively engage fans. By incorporating cutting-edge technologies and interactive elements, brands can foster deeper connections and encourage active participation.

Leveraging Virtual and Augmented Reality

Virtual Reality (VR) and Augmented Reality (AR) have become pivotal in crafting immersive brand experiences:

- Augmented Reality Applications: Brands like IKEA utilize AR to allow customers to visualize furniture in their homes before purchasing, enhancing the shopping experience.

- Virtual Reality Showcases: Automotive companies employ VR to provide virtual test drives, enabling potential buyers to experience vehicles in a controlled, immersive environment.

The AR market is projected to grow from $93.67 billion in 2024 to $1,869.40 billion by 2032, at a CAGR of 45.4%, indicating a significant opportunity for brands to engage with tech-savvy audiences[66].

Gamification: Enhancing Engagement Through Play

Incorporating gamification elements can significantly boost fan interaction:

- Interactive Challenges: Brands can introduce games or challenges that encourage fans to engage, compete, and share their experiences.

- Reward Systems: Implementing point systems or badges for participation can motivate continued engagement and loyalty.

For instance, integrating AR-driven scavenger hunts or VR-based skill challenges can make brand interactions more dynamic and enjoyable.

---

[66] https://www.fortunebusinessinsights.com/augmented-reality-ar-market-102553

EA SPORTS FC 24:
Redefining Immersion Through Innovation

EA Sports is redefining interactive entertainment through technology, AI, and innovation— bringing players closer to their heroes and the sport they love while fueling the future of fandom.

In 2024, EA Sports set a new standard with the launch of *EA SPORTS FC 24*, leveraging cutting-edge technology to elevate player immersion and realism like never before.

HyperMotion V Technology[67]

A standout innovation in EA SPORTS FC 24 is the introduction of HyperMotion V. This technology utilizes volumetric data from over 180 professional matches, capturing the authentic movements of players. By employing stadium cameras, EA Sports translated real- life player kinetics into the virtual realm, resulting in lifelike animations and fluid gameplay that closely mirror actual football dynamics.

---

[67] https://en.wikipedia.org/wiki/EA_Sports_FC_24

Augmented Reality (AR) Coach[68]

To assist players in mastering the game, EA SPORTS FC 24 features an Augmented Reality Coach. This in-game tool provides real-time visual guidance, offering strategic insights and positioning advice during matches. Designed primarily for newcomers, the AR Coach displays visual hints visible only to the player, enhancing decision-making and on-field performance.

Frostbite Engine Enhancements[69]

The game is powered by the advanced Frostbite engine, which delivers lifelike visuals and immersive environments. A notable enhancement includes a GPU-based, compute shader cloth simulation, providing realistic movement and interaction of players' kits. This attention to detail ensures that jerseys and shorts respond authentically to player movements, adding a layer of realism to the gaming experience.

Through these technological advancements, EA Sports has set a new standard in sports gaming, offering players an unparalleled, immersive football experience.

---

[68] https://www.ea.com/en/games/ea-sports-fc/fc-25/news/pitch-notes-fc-25-rush-deep-dive

[69] https://www.ea.com/news/2024-ea-sports-latest-tech-innovations

Strategic Advantage:
Immersive Experiences That Build Brands
and Communities

EA Sports' approach with *EA SPORTS FC 24* and Jordan Brand's *Bred 40 Years* activation are prime examples of how leveraging innovation, immersive experiences, and cultural moments creates long-term strategic advantages. Below is a framework outlining how this approach strengthens the brand, builds loyalty, and fuels fan engagement.

1. Creating Emotional Connection Through Immersion

Why It Matters: Fans don't just want to consume—they want to participate. Interactive and immersive experiences foster deeper emotional engagement, making the brand a key part of their lifestyle.

How It Works:

- EA SPORTS FC 24 integrated AR and hyper-realistic gameplay to bring players closer to the sport, their heroes, and the game's culture.

- Jordan Brand's *Bred 40 Years* activation tapped into nostalgia and heritage through in-person experiences, fueling fan pride and emotional investment.

Strategic Advantage: Emotional connection translates into brand loyalty, increasing retention, engagement, and advocacy.

2. Strengthening Brand Identity and Cultural Relevance

Why It Matters: In order to build fandom a brand must offer more than products—it must represent something bigger. Aligning with cultural moments and trends cements a brand's place in the broader conversation.

How It Works:

- EA Sports' innovative brand activations positioned *EA SPORTS FC 24* as the future of gaming entertainment, keeping the franchise culturally relevant.

- Jordan Brand's *Bred 40 Years* campaign capitalized on Super Bowl weekend—its first-ever activation during the event—to engage new audiences and amplify its cultural presence.

Strategic Advantage: A strong brand identity differentiates the brand in a competitive market and ensures long-term relevance.

3. Amplifying Reach and Engagement Through Social and Digital Integration

Why It Matters: Fans are the most effective marketers. Creating experiences designed for social sharing expands reach and deepens engagement organically.

How It Works:

- EA SPORTS FC 24 leveraged digital activations and influencer collaborations to fuel global conversations.
- Jordan Brand integrated influencer-led storytelling, real-time social engagement, and early-access drops to generate buzz.

Strategic Advantage: Fans become brand ambassadors, driving organic word-of-mouth marketing and increasing customer acquisition.

4. Driving Sales Through Exclusivity and Participation

Why It Matters: Scarcity and participation fuel demand. When fans feel like they are part of something exclusive, they are more likely to engage and convert.

How It Works:

- EA Sports used exclusive in-game features, collaborations, and interactive activations to drive sales.
- Jordan Brand's early-release strategy and thematic in-store experiences created urgency, boosting both hype and sell-through.

Strategic Advantage: Exclusivity strengthens brand equity, boosts immediate sales, and drives long-term brand value.

5. Fostering a Loyal and Engaged Community

Why It Matters: A brand's most valuable asset isn't its product—it's its community. Creating spaces for fans to interact, engage, and co-create builds long-term loyalty.

How It Works:

- EA Sports leveraged its deep community-driven approach with social platforms, Discord servers, and in-game communities to maintain engagement.

- Jordan Brand created live and digital spaces for sneakerheads, athletes, and cultural influencers to share their passion for the Bred colorway.

Strategic Advantage: A highly engaged community fuels repeat purchases, lifetime value, and brand advocacy.

Key Takeaway: Turning Engagement into Long-Term Brand Power

Brands that prioritize immersive, community-driven experiences don't just win short-term engagement; they build movements. EA Sports and Jordan Brand demonstrate how experiential marketing, exclusivity, and cultural storytelling turn fans into lifelong brand advocates—driving revenue, cultural relevance, and sustained growth.

For any brand looking to build lasting impact, the playbook is clear: *innovate, immerse, and invite fans into the journey.*

Brand Storytelling Through Events: Bringing Your Message to Life

Events aren't just about gathering people—they're a platform for storytelling. The most powerful brand activations don't just entertain; they immerse fans in a narrative that deepens emotional connection and reinforces brand identity.

To stand out, brands must go beyond surface-level engagement. Every element—from the environment to the programming, from interactive touchpoints to digital integration—should serve a singular purpose: bringing your brand's story to life.

How to Craft Unforgettable Brand Storytelling Through Events

1. Create an Immersive Narrative – The best events feel like stepping into a story. Whether it's an activation that transports fans to a different era, a multi-sensory experience that brings innovation to life, or an intimate setting that fosters personal connection, the environment should be an extension of the brand's message.

2. Blend Physical & Digital Storytelling – Social media is where experiences live forever. Leverage AR filters, interactive apps, and real-time social integration to allow fans to co-create and amplify the story beyond the event itself.

3. Evoke Emotion Through Personalization – The most impactful brand experiences make fans feel something. Whether it's *nostalgia, empowerment, or exclusivity,* storytelling should be crafted to trigger an emotional response that lingers. Make them see themselves in the experience.

From Storytelling to Innovation:
The Next Evolution of Super Events

The most iconic brand activations are built on a foundation of storytelling and innovation. Events should evolve beyond traditional formats and embrace *technology, interactivity, and digital-first experiences* to stay relevant in today's hyper-connected world.

The brands that win are the ones that don't just tell a story but invite fans to be part of it. What's your brand's story—and how will you make it unforgettable?

Creating Exclusivity:
Elevating Fan Loyalty and Brand Value

Exclusivity and scarcity is a powerful strategy for deepening fan loyalty and driving brand desirability. When fans feel like they are part of an insider experience, they engage more, advocate more, and form a deeper emotional bond with the brand.

How to Create Exclusivity That Drives Engagement[70]

1. VIP Access & Limited Invitations – Offer early access to products, exclusive meet-and-greets, or invite-only experiences that make fans feel valued. The feeling of being part of something rare fuels anticipation and demand.

2. Event-Only Collectibles – Limited-edition merchandise or exclusive in-event drops create an added incentive to participate, while also giving fans tangible proof of their membership in the brand's inner circle.

---

[70] https://zatap.io/loyalty-events/

3.   Personalized Invitations – Personalization transforms an invite from an announcement into an experience. A VIP event invitation should build excitement and reinforce the fan's connection to the brand.

Using Technology to Enhance Exclusivity

- Contactless Innovation – Brands are integrating near-field communication (NFC) and interactive microsites to create digital-first invitations that offer seamless access to exclusive content, event perks, or personalized experiences.

- Interactive Video Invites – Video invitations from brand ambassadors, athletes, or executives add a human touch, building hype and making fans feel personally invited into the experience.

Coachella: The Blueprint for Cultural Influence

Coachella isn't just a music festival—it's a global cultural moment powered by influencer-driven storytelling. By strategically partnering with creators, the festival transforms attendees into brand amplifiers, flooding social media with aspirational content that extends its reach far beyond the desert. This approach has turned Coachella into more than an event—it's a status symbol and a must-experience phenomenon.

Influencer collaborations are a force multiplier for exclusivity. The right partnerships can take an intimate VIP experience and give it a global impact.

- Authenticity That Fans Trust – Influencers bring credibility and a relatable voice, making the brand experience feel organic, not staged.

- Expanding Reach & Creating Demand – Influencers and brand ambassadors introduce new audiences to exclusive events, turning limited activations into must-attend cultural moments.

- Built-In Content Creation – The best brand activations aren't just about what happens at the event—they're about the stories that get told after the event. Influencer-generated content gives brands extended exposure and a fresh perspective that resonates with fans.

The Bottom Line: Exclusivity and scarcity isn't just about limiting access—it's about creating experiences that feel rare, special, and deeply personal. When done right, they strengthen fandom, build community, and turn moments into movements.

From Cultural Influence to Intentional Brand Experiences

Cultural relevance and influencer partnerships can ignite interest, but truly impactful events require more than just buzz—they demand intentional design. The most successful activations seamlessly blend brand storytelling with immersive, thoughtfully curated experiences that leave a lasting impression.

This is where event design and branding come into play. Every element of the event, from venue selection to post-event engagement, should reflect the brand's identity and reinforce its message. A well-executed event isn't just an experience—it's a statement, a feeling, and a memory that fans carry forward.

Turning Brand Storytelling Into Immersive Experiences

Cultural influence and hype can spark initial interest, but truly unforgettable events go beyond spectacle—they immerse fans in a brand's world and leave a lasting imprint. To achieve this, brand leaders must approach **event design with precision**, ensuring every element aligns with their identity and delivers an experience that deepens emotional connections.

Designing for Impact: Bringing a Brand to Life

A well-executed event is a tangible expression of the brand—every detail should reinforce its purpose, values, and aesthetic. Here's how to build that consistency:

- Venue Selection: The setting should feel like an extension of the brand, amplifying its story and enhancing the fan experience.

- Aesthetic Coherence: From color palettes to logo placement, visual consistency builds brand recognition and elevates the event's credibility.

- Atmosphere & Ambience: Lighting, music, and decor should create an environment that evokes emotion and keeps fans engaged.

Take Apple's product launches—every keynote event is an immersive representation of the brand's innovation. The sleek stage design, minimalist visuals, and precise storytelling ensure that attendees and global viewers alike experience Apple's DNA in real time.

Keeping the Momentum Alive: Engagement Beyond the Event

A successful event isn't just about the day it happens—it should serve as a launchpad for continued brand interaction. Engagement should be carefully structured before, during, and after the event to maintain relevance and maximize impact.

How to Extend the Experience: Lessons from Gaming & Esports

Gaming and esports have redefined what it means to engage an audience beyond the physical arena. These industries have mastered multi-platform experiences, ensuring that live events are just the beginning of a longer, more immersive journey for fans worldwide.

Here's how top gaming and esports brands extend the event experience at a **global scale**:

Pre-Event Hype: Build anticipation with teaser trailers, exclusive content drops, and collaborations with top gaming influencers.

- *Example: Riot Games and the League of Legends World Championship*—months before the tournament, Riot builds anticipation with cinematic trailers, custom in-game skins, and music collaborations (like their Worlds anthem releases), engaging fans long before the first match.

Live Streaming & Social Media Engagement: Offer immersive real-time experiences beyond in-person attendance.

- *Example: The Fortnite World Cup*—Epic Games ensured that millions of fans worldwide could experience the event live through interactive Twitch streams, in-game viewing parties, and exclusive event-themed content drops within Fortnite itself.

Post-Event Follow-Ups: Sustain engagement by turning key moments into shareable, evergreen content.

- *Example: VALORANT Champions Tour (VCT)*—game developer Riot Games capitalizes on post-event engagement with cinematic recaps, highlight reels, and exclusive behind-the-scenes interviews, ensuring the hype carries over into the next season.

Key Takeaway:
Turning Events into Year-Round Movements

A live event is just the start. Brands that build anticipation, integrate real-time digital experiences, and sustain engagement afterward transform moments into movements.

Gaming and esports prove that live events don't end when the lights go out. Pre-event hype, live streaming, and post-event content keep fans engaged long after. By adopting gaming-inspired strategies—interactive content, influencer collaborations, and exclusive drops—brands can turn single events into lasting fan experiences.

Measuring Success: Analyzing the Impact and ROI of Your Event

To evaluate an event's effectiveness, brands should focus on key performance indicators (KPIs) that align with their objectives. These metrics provide insights into audience engagement and the event's overall impact.

Key Metrics to Assess:

- Attendance and Participation: Monitor the number of attendees and their engagement levels. High attendance coupled with active participation indicates a successful event—which can be measured by an increase in average spend per ticket.

- Social Media Metrics: Track hashtag usage, mentions, shares, and overall sentiment. A surge in positive social media activity reflects heightened brand visibility and audience engagement—which will result in stronger brand awareness and loyalty.

- Brand Sentiment and Feedback: Utilize surveys and sentiment analysis to gauge attendee satisfaction and perceptions. Positive feedback can affirm the event's success, while constructive criticism offers areas for improvement.

- Sales and Conversions: Analyze the direct impact on revenue, including ticket sales, merchandise purchases, and new customer acquisitions. An uptick in sales post-event signifies effective audience conversion.

Illustrative Example: IEM Katowice—Breaking Records and Setting New Benchmarks

The Intel Extreme Masters tournament, Katowice 2025, set a new standard for Counter-Strike 2 esports viewership, proving the power of live events in growing fandom, driving engagement, and elevating brand partnerships.

- 1.3 million peak viewers – the most-watched non-major Counter-Strike tournament in history (+33.7% YoY), highlighting the power of driving product-centric brand campaigns.

- Average viewership increased by 32.6% – demonstrating a strong fanbase eager for live competition and a highly-captive audience, retention rates are key indicators.

- Total hours watched up 24.7% – proving extended engagement and a deeper connection with the audience.

These record-breaking numbers highlight how a well-executed event can elevate a game's ecosystem, increase its cultural relevance, and solidify brand loyalty among fans.

The Role of Marketing in Driving Engagement and Growth

Strategic marketing initiatives are pivotal in amplifying an event's reach and impact. By crafting compelling narratives and leveraging multiple platforms, brands can:

- Increase Ticket Sales and Attendance: Effective promotion and pre-event hype create anticipation, leading to higher ticket sales and packed venues.

- Enhance Viewership and Streaming Hours: Engaging digital content and strategic partnerships attract larger audiences to live broadcasts and streaming platforms, maximizing reach.

- Expand Audience and Brand Reach: Consistent, targeted marketing efforts help attract new fans, fostering community growth and increasing brand equity.

Why It Matters

IEM Katowice 2025 is a prime example of how esports events are evolving into global spectacles that drive revenue, engagement, and brand loyalty. By investing in experiential marketing, brands can build unforgettable moments, sustain long-term fan engagement, and solidify their position as cultural leaders in their industries.

The Ultimate Brand Leader Fandom Checklist

Creating unforgettable fan activations isn't just about throwing events—it's about building deep emotional connections, leveraging innovation, and making data-driven decisions. Use this checklist to ensure your brand is delivering high-impact experiences that keep fans engaged and loyal.

1. Listen to Your Fans and Analyze the Market

Fans don't just want to support a brand—they want to be part of it. The best insights don't come from boardrooms; they come from your community.

- Monitor digital platforms and social media for fan feedback and emerging trends.
- Track what content and experiences are gaining popularity in your industry.
- Analyze how other brands are leveraging technology to enhance fan engagement.
- Actively invite and integrate fan input into your activations to strengthen loyalty.

2. Be Innovative—Challenge the Status Quo

New technologies are reshaping the way fans engage. To stay ahead, your brand must continuously push boundaries.

- Audit your current technology stack and content strategy—what's working, what's outdated?
- Explore how marketing, design, and engineering teams can collaborate for innovative activations.
- Stay ahead of industry trends by researching cutting-edge fan experiences.
- Provide spaces for fan feedback and be receptive to their evolving needs.

3. Trigger Emotions—Make Fans Feel Something

People don't remember facts—they remember feelings. Emotionally charged experiences create lasting impressions and drive deeper engagement.

- Craft activations that evoke excitement, nostalgia, and pride.
- Ensure that every campaign has a clear purpose—no fluff, no fillers.
- Use storytelling to make fans feel connected to the brand on a personal level.

4. Use Data to Make Smarter Decisions

Great activations aren't just creative—they're strategic. Fan data provides valuable insights into behavior, preferences, and trends.

- Capture and analyze fan engagement data across digital and live experiences.
- Identify key trends and patterns that inform future marketing strategies.
- Use real-time data to refine and optimize activations for maximum impact.
- Continuously test and iterate based on performance insights.

5. Build a Long-Term Community, Not Just One-Off Moments

Fandom isn't about a single campaign—it's about sustained connection. The most successful brands keep fans engaged beyond a single event or activation.

- Create fan-centric platforms (forums, Discord servers, exclusive memberships) to keep the conversation going.
- Offer consistent value through exclusive content, behind-the-scenes access, and loyalty rewards.
- Foster user-generated content by empowering fans to share their experiences and stories.
- Reinforce your brand's presence in their lives with ongoing touchpoints, not just periodic promotions.

Final Thought: Build a Movement, Not Just a Moment

Fans are the heartbeat of every successful brand. Every decision, activation, and campaign should center around them—what they love, what they feel, and how they engage. The brands that listen, innovate, and create emotional connections and gain more than just buyers..

Memorable events and activations are more than marketing tactics—they are catalysts for brand growth, shaping culture and fueling fandom. By leveraging immersive storytelling, strategic exclusivity, and sustained engagement, brands can turn fleeting moments into movements that drive loyalty, advocacy, and long-term success.

The brands that win don't just show up. They create experiences that leave a mark. So, the real question is—are you ready to build something that lasts?

CHAPTER 10
BUILT TO LAST.
THE TRANSFORMATIONAL BLUEPRINT FOR WINNING BRANDS

In the end, every brand faces a choice: chase relevance, or create resonance. One fades fast. The other lasts forever.

Building a brand people remember is no longer enough. The real challenge—and the real opportunity—is to build something they can *feel*. Something they *stand by*, not just stand in line for. Something they *carry with them*, long after the campaign ends or the product wears out. That's the difference between a brand that's momentary—and one that leaves a legacy.

Legacy is built the same way the strongest human relationships are: through trust, shared values, and emotional alignment. It's not just what your brand says—it's how it makes people feel. And more importantly, how it makes them feel about *how* they feel.

Researcher John Gottman[71] calls this "meta-emotion"—our feelings about our feelings. In his decades-long study of relationships, Gottman found that couples with aligned meta-emotional styles—shared ways of expressing happiness, frustration, excitement—were the ones that endured. Not because they avoided hardship, but because they navigated it together.

The same is true for fandom. It's easy to attract attention when things are going well. But lasting brands—the ones that shape culture and stand the test of time—stay emotionally aligned with their audience, even through uncertainty, setbacks, and change.

---

[71] **Gottman, J. M., Katz, L. F., & Hooven, C. (1997).** *Meta-Emotion: How Families Communicate Emotionally*. Lawrence Erlbaum Associates.

Ask yourself:

- Does your brand only show up when it's convenient? Or does it show up when it counts?
- Do your fans see your mission as their own?
- Do they feel seen, heard, and understood?

Fandom isn't about the flash of a product drop or a perfectly polished ad. It's about building a relationship with your audience that's resilient, real, and rooted in something deeper. Because when people feel emotionally connected to your brand—not just what you sell, but *why you exist*—they don't just stick around. They advocate. They defend. They *belong*.

This chapter is your call to rise above the noise—to stop playing for awareness and start building for impact. The brands that win the future aren't the ones chasing trends. They're the ones forging unshakable bonds, grounded in purpose, fueled by emotion, and carried by a community that refuses to let them fade.

Because at the end of the day, brands come and go. But legacies live on.

Understanding Fans on a Deeper Level

To create genuine, lasting connections, brands must understand their fans beyond just demographics. What drives them? What excites them? What frustrates them? What do they expect from you?

This isn't a one-time research project—it's an ongoing commitment. It means:

- Listening—Social media, surveys, direct conversations, and community insights.
- Analyzing Engagement—Tracking patterns, responses, and behaviors.
- Responding & Adapting—Adjusting strategies based on real fan feedback.

Winning Brandss don't just sell products—they create emotional resonance. They understand their fans' values, hopes, and struggles—and they show up consistently.

Will Your Fans Stick with You When It Gets Hard?

No relationship is perfect. Even the strongest brands hit turbulence—a failed product launch, a PR crisis, or a cultural misstep.

The real question is: Will your fans stand by you when things go wrong?

If you've built real emotional equity—if they feel heard, valued, and aligned with your brand's deeper mission—they won't just stick around... they'll fight for you.

Cultivating loyalty isn't about never making mistakes. It's about *building a foundation* strong enough to survive when you do make them.

And that's what this chapter is about: building something so real, so deep, and so emotionally powerful that your fans don't just engage—they belong.

Consistency Wins: The Foundation of Trust & Fandom

Trust isn't built overnight—it's *earned through consistency*. The brands that truly win are the ones that show up again and again, delivering value, staying true to their mission, and engaging with their audience in meaningful ways.

This isn't just about posting regularly on social media—it's about creating a pattern of engagement that fans can rely on—your brand needs to be there when and where they need it. Whether it's through personalized emails, live events, interactive content, or real-time responses, your brand needs to be a consistent presence in your fans' lives.

Inconsistency kills momentum. A brand that disappears for weeks or months at a time loses trust. Fans don't just forget—they move on. Loyalty is fueled by regular, intentional touchpoints that reinforce your brand's message, values, and emotional connection.

The Power of Consistency in Brand Identity

Look at the most iconic brands in the world—Nike, Apple, Coca-Cola. They've built their legacies on unwavering consistency. Coca-Cola's red color and script logo have been instantly recognizable since 1886—nearly 140 years of branding dominance!

And consumers notice.

81% of consumers say brand consistency plays a key role in their loyalty[72]. That's not a coincidence—it's a direct result of brands delivering a seamless, reliable experience across every touchpoint.

Cut Through the Noise & Stay Top of Mind

In a world where millions of brands are competing for attention, being distinctive can mean the difference between being remembered and being forgotten.

- A clear, recognizable brand voice.
- A steady content cadence across platforms.
- Messaging that aligns with values and mission.
- Engagement that never feels forced or transactional.

The brands that *show up, engage, and deliver* time and time again are the ones that win the long game. If you want to build an epic fandom—one that stands by your brand through thick and thin—consistency isn't optional. It's essential.

So, are you in for the long haul? Your fans are waiting.

Personalization: The Key to Fandom That Lasts

We all love hearing our name. It's a simple, yet powerful truth—because personalization makes us feel seen. And in today's world, fans don't just want to follow a brand; they want to feel like they're part of it.

The brands that win loyalty don't treat fans like an audience—they treat them like individuals. Personalization isn't just about using someone's first name in an email. It's about curating experiences, content, and perks that make fans feel valued, included, and connected on a personal level.

With AI and analytics, brands can tailor recommendations, rewards, and interactions in ways that feel effortless—but deeply meaningful. The more personal and relevant the experience, the stronger the emotional connection.

---

[72] https://content-whale.com/blog/importance-of-content-consistency-for-branding/#:~:text=With%20countless%20brands%20vying%20for,important%20for%20their%20loyalty%E2%80%8B.

Brands That Get It Right: Starbucks & Netflix

Starbucks

- The brand's gamified rewards app keeps fans engaged, integrating personalized drink recommendations, order history, and location-based perks. When the rewards system launched, revenue soared to $2.56 billion, and today, the app drives 22% of all U.S. Starbucks sales[73]—because customers feel like their experience is uniquely theirs.

Netflix

- Beyond simply offering just personalized recommendations, Netflix actually actively involves their fans in the experience of advertising the new show[74]. To promote *Black Mirror: Joan Is Awful*, the platform invited fans to create their own personalized billboards, using AI to generate posters featuring their own names and faces. The result? Massive social engagement, viral buzz, and an audience that felt like they were part of the show itself.

Beyond Digital: Creating Personalized Fan Experiences IRL

Real fandom isn't built-in algorithms alone. Brands should extend personalization into the physical world, offering:

1. VIP events & fan clubs—where superfans get exclusive access.
2. Customized merchandise & experiences—turning everyday fans into insiders.
3. Surprise & delight moments—because unexpected personal touches create unbreakable loyalty.

The Takeaway? Make Every Fan Feel Like the Only Fan.

A fan who feels valued doesn't just stick around—they shout your name from the rooftops. They become brand ambassadors, sharing their experiences and bringing others into the fold. So, how are you making your fans feel like they belong to your brand?

---

[73] https://www.gwi.com/blog/personalized-marketing-works
[74] https://www.gwi.com/blog/personalized-marketing-works

Rewarding Loyalty: Turning Fans into Lifelong Advocates

Loyal fans deserve to be recognized. The more valued they feel, the more likely they are to stay engaged, advocate for your brand, and bring others into the fold.

This doesn't just mean discounts or giveaways—it's about creating meaningful rewards that tap into emotional connection, exclusivity, and community.

Loyalty That Drives Engagement & Growth

According to the Harvard Business Review[75] emotionally connected fans are more than twice as valuable as highly satisfied fans. Why? Because they don't just like the brand—they identify with it. They stay for reasons like:

1. A sense of belonging
2. Aligning with their personal values
3. Feeling like an insider

How to Reward Fans & Deepen Connection

- Exclusive Access & VIP Perks – Early product drops, invite-only events, and behind-the-scenes content keep fans engaged and feeling special.

- Public Recognition & Fan Spotlights – Acknowledging fans on social media, featuring their content, or creating personalized thank-you messages builds a deep emotional bond.

- Gamification & Status-Based Rewards – Leaderboards, milestone perks, and tiered memberships create aspiration-driven engagement—fans stay involved to unlock the next level.

---

[75] https://www.cheetahdigital.com/blog/5-ways-loyalty-program-gives-competitive-edge/

Brands That Master Loyalty

Delta SkyMiles: Loyalty That Keeps Fans Flying

Delta Air Lines has built one of the most successful and highly lucrative[76] loyalty programs in the travel industry. In 2023, Delta reported a record operating revenue of $54.7 billion, with premium and non-ticket revenue accounting for 55% of the total.

Delta's success comes from making loyalty aspirational and habit-forming. Elite status tiers, rollover miles, and strategic partnerships (like American Express co-branded credit cards) ensure that travelers always have an incentive to stay within the Delta ecosystem. The higher the loyalty tier, the more exclusive the perks—ranging from complimentary upgrades to access to premium lounges, turning buyers into believers.

Marriott Bonvoy: Turning Stays into Lifestyle Experiences

Marriott's Bonvoy program isn't just about hotel stays—it's about creating unforgettable travel experiences. As of 2024, Marriott Bonvoy has surpassed 200 million members[77], maintaining its status as the largest hotel loyalty program globally.

---

[76] https://ir.delta.com/news/news-details/2025/Delta-Air-Lines-Announces-December-Quarter-and-Full-Year-2024-Financial-Results/default.aspx

[77] https://skift.com/2024/02/26/marriott-bonvoy-adds-200-millionth-member-as-hotel-loyalty-race-heats-up/

The key to Bonvoy's success? Personalized rewards and tiered exclusivity. Members earn points for stays and everyday spending, unlocking perks like suite upgrades, late checkouts, and once-in-a-lifetime experiences through Marriott Bonvoy Moments. This strategy has positioned Marriott as not just a hospitality brand but as a lifestyle brand that fuels travel dreams and aspirations.

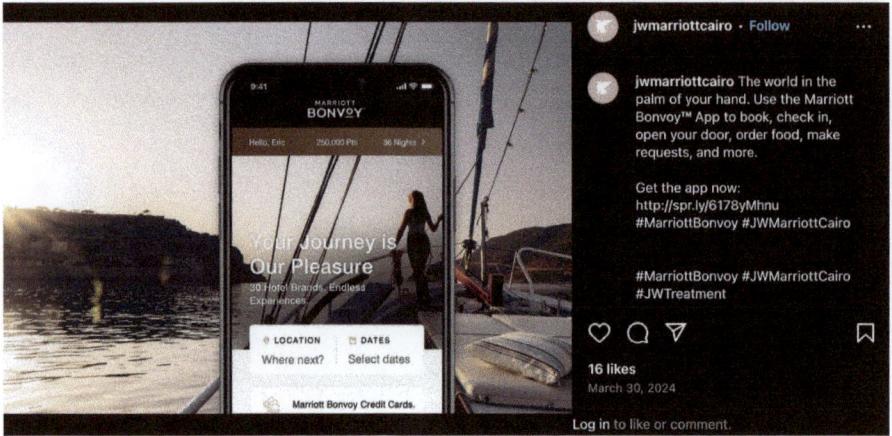

Loyalty Isn't a Program—It's a Mindset

Fans who feel valued and celebrated aren't just repeat customers—they become evangelists. When your brand rewards loyalty in a way that resonates emotionally, fans don't just engage more—they live and breathe your brand. Ask yourself: Are you giving your fans a reason to stay for life?

Fostering Belonging: Turning Fans into a Community

Fans don't just want to engage with a brand—they want to belong to something bigger than themselves. A strong fan community transforms passive supporters into active participants, creating an ecosystem where people feel connected, valued, and inspired.

When brands facilitate spaces where fans can connect with each other, rather than just the brand, they unlock a deeper level of engagement. This isn't about pushing content—it's about creating platforms where fans drive the conversation, shape the culture, and fuel the momentum.

From Audience to Community: Creating Shared Spaces

Loyalty isn't just about transactions—it's about *identity*. Fans don't just follow a brand; they adopt it as part of their lifestyle. That's why brands need to curate spaces that foster genuine connection and belonging.

Real-World Examples of Building Fan Communities

Online Communities & Social Groups: Esports & Discord – The Power of Always-On Engagement

- In esports and gaming, online communities aren't just an extension of the experience—they are the heart of the fandom.

- Take League of Legends: Riot Games has built one of the most engaged gaming communities on Discord, where fans discuss strategies, get real-time game updates, and interact with pro players and influencers.

- By fostering *always-on engagement,* Riot turns casual players into deeply invested fans, ensuring that even when they're not playing, they're still part of the ecosystem—watching streams, debating updates, and hyping the next tournament.

Live Events & Fan Meetups: Pokémon GO – Bringing Digital Fandom into the Real World

- The Pokémon GO Tour is a perfect example of turning an online game into an in-person fan movement.

- Niantic, the developers of Pokémon GO, host global live events where thousands of fans physically gather to explore cities, catch rare Pokémon, and connect with other players.

- A game that transcends the screen—fostering lifelong friendships, shared nostalgia, and a sense of adventure that fans can't get anywhere else.

UGC Campaigns: TikTok & The Viral Power of Fan-Driven Trends

- TikTok creators have redefined brand engagement by blurring the line between consumer and creator.

- Take Chipotle's #GuacDance challenge—inspired by National Avocado Day, it encouraged fans to create fun dance videos for free guac. The result? 250K video submissions in six days and over 800M impressions.

- TikTok UGC isn't just marketing—it's fans taking ownership of a brand and making it part of their identity, turning them from passive consumers into cultural ambassadors.

A well-nurtured community becomes self-sustaining, where fans engage with one another, bring in new members, and drive organic brand growth.

Technology: Supercharging the Fan Experience

While brand storytelling and exclusivity build loyalty, technology elevates it. Smart brands integrate cutting-edge tools to enhance the fan journey, making interactions seamless, immersive, and unforgettable.

AI-Powered Personalization: FACEIT's Minerva AI – The Future of Tailored Esports Experiences

In the competitive gaming world, personalization is key to player retention. FACEIT, one of the leading esports platforms, has revolutionized the fan and player experience with Minerva AI.

- A proprietary AI tool that analyzes player behavior, skill levels, and preferences to deliver customized tournament recommendations, matchmaking, and anti-toxicity measures.

- By leveraging predictive analytics, Minerva AI ensures that every player's experience is tailored to their skill level and interests, reducing churn and keeping the community highly engaged.

Augmented & Virtual Reality: Meta x Ray-Ban – Bringing Fans Into the Future

Meta's collaboration with Ray-Ban has created a new era of hands-free, immersive engagement with its Ray-Ban Meta Smart Glasses.

- Fans can livestream their experiences, capture POV content instantly, and even access real-time translations and AI-powered assistance—creating an **augmented** reality experience that brings digital fandom into everyday life.

- Imagine attending a live sports game and getting player stats through your glasses in real time—this is where AR-driven fan engagement is heading.

- Sales Performance[78]: Since their launch in October 2023, over 2 million units of Ray-Ban Meta smart glasses have been sold, surpassing initial expectations.

- Production Expansion[79]: In response to high demand, EssilorLuxottica plans to increase production capacity to 10 million units annually by the end of 2026.

- Retail Success[80]: The Ray-Ban Meta smart glasses have become the top-selling product in 60% of Ray-Ban stores across Europe, the Middle East, and Africa.

These figures underscore the growing consumer interest and market traction of the Meta and Ray-Ban smart glasses collaboration.

Gamification & Rewards Apps: Starbucks Rewards – The Gold Standard of Fan Loyalty

Starbucks has gamified loyalty like no other brand with its Starbucks Rewards app—a system where customers earn stars for every purchase, unlocking free drinks, exclusive menu items, and VIP perks.

- **Instant gratification through gamification**—from personalized challenges that encourage repeat visits to seasonal promotions that drive engagement.

- As of December 31, 2023, Starbucks reported that **31% of total transactions at U.S. company-operated stores were made via the app**[81], up from 27% in the previous year.

---

[78] https://www.theverge.com/news/613292/meta-ray-ban-2-million-10-million-capacity-subscription-essilor-luxottica-earnings

[79] https://www.reuters.com/technology/essilorluxottica-boost-production-capacity-smart-glasses-2025-02-13/

[80] https://www.uploadvr.com/ray-ban-meta-glasses-top-selling-emea/

[81] https://www.geekwire.com/2024/starbucks-mobile-orders-surpass-30-of-total-transactions-at-u-s-stores-for-the-first-time/

- Additionally, the Starbucks Rewards program boasted 34.3 million active U.S. members, accounting for nearly 60% of sales at company-operated U.S. stores in the most recent quarter[82].

This strategy has turned casual customers into devoted brand advocates, demonstrating the power of a well-executed gamified rewards program.

A brand that builds a community isn't just selling a product—it's shaping a culture. And when fans feel like they truly belong, they don't just engage more—they bring others along for the ride. Are you giving them a reason to stay, connect, and champion your brand?

Elevating Fan Experiences[83]

These in-person fan experiences are fantastic ways to enhance engagement, create shareable moments, and immerse attendees in your brand's world. Let's refine and strengthen each concept with clarity, real-world impact, and seamless execution strategies.

1. Photo Experience:

In the era of social media dominance, every event should be optimized for shareability. Fans love capturing moments, and when done right, a photo experience can turn them into organic brand ambassadors.

How to Execute It Effectively:

- Strategic Placement: Position well-lit, branded photo stations in high-traffic areas to maximize visibility and engagement.
- Integrated Branding: Include logos, campaign hashtags, and event-specific overlays so that every shared post extends your brand's reach.
- Interactive Enhancements: Use touchless LED kiosks where fans can add digital props, place themselves next to their favorite athletes or celebrities, and instantly share their customized photos via email or social media.

---

[82] https://www.customerexperiencedive.com/news/starbucks-rewards-loyalty-q3-personalization/706212/

[83] https://bluewatertech.com/4-ideas-for-creating-the-ultimate-fan-experience/

Why It Works:

Fans love exclusive, interactive experiences, and a well-designed photo station turns every attendee into a micro-influencer. Studies show that over 70% of consumers are more likely to trust user-generated content over traditional advertising—so why not let them create the content for you?

2. RFID or NFC Credentials: Elevating Fan Convenience & Personalization

The magic of RFID (Radio Frequency Identification) and NFC (Near Field Communication) technology isn't just in streamlining event logistics—it's in creating seamless, personalized fan experiences. Disney's MagicBand system set the gold standard, transforming every guest's visit into a frictionless journey.

Ways to Implement This at Your Event:

- Frictionless Entry & Payments: Attendees can use RFID wristbands or NFC-enabled passes for ticketless entry, cashless transactions, and quick access to exclusive areas.

- VIP Access & Gamification: Give top-tier guests access to premium lounges, early merchandise drops, or VIP meet-and-greets, enhancing the value of upgraded experiences.

- Interactive Engagements: Use location-based activation—such as triggering personalized welcome messages, playing custom music, or unlocking exclusive digital content when fans enter certain areas.

Why It Works:

Beyond the convenience factor, RFID increases attendee spending by 20%, as guests are more likely to make impulse purchases when the transaction process is seamless. Moreover, the data collected from these interactions provides powerful insights into fan behavior, helping brands refine future activations.

3. Projection-Mapping: Bringing Your Brand to Life

Projection mapping is more than just a cool visual effect—it's an immersive storytelling tool that turns any event into a *sensory-driven spectacle*.

How to Use It at Your Event:

- Transform Venues & Cityscapes: Light up entire buildings, arenas, or landmarks with dynamic visuals, making the event feel larger-than-life.

- Live Engagement & Entertainment: Use projection mapping to display live social media feeds, audience-generated content, or interactive animations that respond to movement.

- Partner & Sponsor Integration: Feature sponsor advertisements in an engaging way—rather than static banners, showcase dynamic, eye-catching projections that blend seamlessly into the event.

Why It Works:

A well-executed projection mapping display not only wows attendees but extends event storytelling beyond the physical space. Research shows that dynamic digital displays capture 400% more attention than static imagery, proving that immersive visuals can significantly enhance brand recall.

Bringing It All Together:

Each of these activations—photo experiences, RFID/NFC integration, and projection mapping—elevates the fan experience from passive to interactive. They tap into key emotional drivers: *exclusivity, personalization, and immersion*, ensuring that fans don't just attend an event but actively participate in it.

The brands that master in-person experiences don't just create moments, they create movements.

Telling the Right Stories

Storytelling is at the heart of fan engagement—it keeps your brand narrative alive and ensures your audience remains emotionally invested. Whether through brand history, behind-the-scenes content, or fan-driven testimonials, great storytelling invites fans into your world and makes them feel like a part of something bigger.

But storytelling isn't just about sharing content—it's about sharing the right content. To truly resonate, your brand's narrative must align with who you are, what your audience cares about, and what you can offer them. The best stories live at the intersection of these three elements.

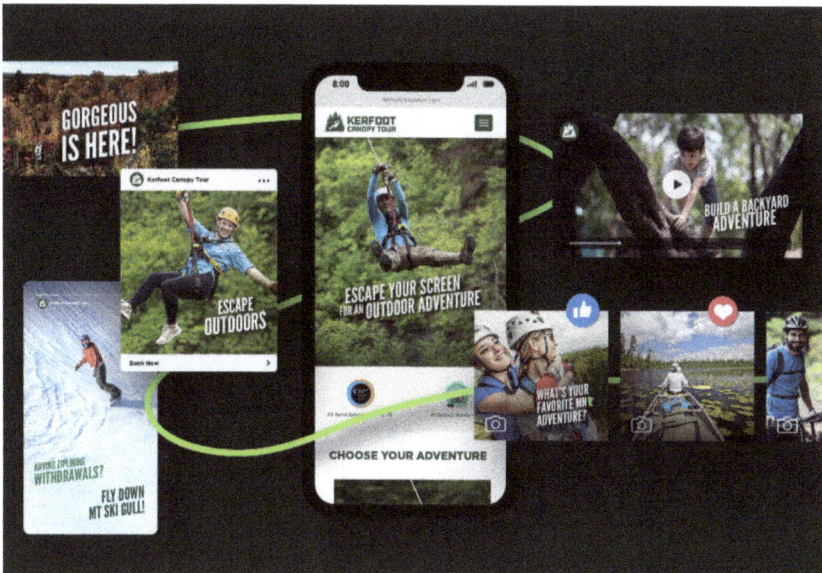

Before you hit "post" on your next campaign, take a step back. Are you telling a story that reflects your brand's identity? Does it tap into your fans' needs and aspirations? And most importantly, does it provide them with something meaningful?

Let's break it down—here's how to determine what story your brand should tell[84].

How to Determine the Right Story for Your Brand

The most impactful brand stories don't just inform—they connect. They capture attention, inspire action, and foster loyalty. But to stand out in the endless sea of content, your story must live at the intersection of three critical elements:

1. Your Identity – Your mission, vision, and values define your brand's identity. What do you stand for? What's your purpose beyond selling a product? A strong brand story starts with authenticity.

2. Your Audience" – To be relevant, you need to deeply understand your fans. What are their aspirations, challenges, and desires? What do they care about right now? Your brand must align with their evolving needs and values.

3. **Your Promise** – Your story should make it clear how your brand enhances your audience's life. Whether it's inspiration, empowerment, entertainment, or problem-solving, your narrative must provide real value.

When you craft stories that connect these three points, you're not just marketing—you're creating an experience your audience wants to be part of.

Transparency and Authenticity: Building Trust Through Honesty

In today's market, consumers are increasingly discerning and value honesty and authenticity from the brands they support. Being transparent about business decisions, openly addressing mistakes, and showcasing the human side of your brand are pivotal in fostering trust and loyalty. Authenticity should be the cornerstone of all brand communications, ensuring that fans recognize your brand as genuine and aligned with their values.

---

[84] https://blend.travel/blog/storytelling/

Recent studies underscore the importance of transparency:

- Trustworthiness and Transparency: A 2022 survey revealed that 60% of consumers worldwide consider trustworthiness and transparency as the most important traits of a brand, up from 55% in 2021[85].

- Consumer Expectations: Research indicates that 72% of consumers find transparency important or extremely important, with 79% desiring brands to exceed mandatory disclosure requirements[86].

These findings highlight that transparency isn't merely a corporate responsibility—it's a strategic advantage. Brands that operate with integrity and communicate openly are more likely to cultivate a loyal fan base that trusts and champions them.

Fans Build Brands. Listen to Them.

A brand that doesn't listen is a brand that won't stand the test of time. The most successful brands don't dictate—they co-create. Fans aren't just consumers; they're collaborators, culture drivers, and your most valuable source of insight.

Listening isn't passive. It's an active strategy. The brands that win are the ones that take real action—gathering feedback, making changes, and showing fans that their voices shape the experience.

The message is clear: *Engage. Adapt. Evolve.* The moment you stop listening, you stop growing. But if you continuously put fans at the center, they'll take your brand further than you ever imagined.

This isn't just marketing. This is fandom. This is the future.

The Power of Fandom in Building

The brands that lead, inspire, and endure are the ones that create a deep emotional connection with their audience. The shift from customers to fans is the ultimate unlock—turning a business into a brand that shapes culture, commands influence, and drives lasting loyalty.

---

[85] https://www.statista.com/statistics/1332294/trustworthiness-transparency-in-marketing/
[86] https://www.business.com/articles/leading-with-transparency/

Fandom isn't built on transactions; it's built on trust, authenticity, and shared experiences. The brands that embrace this shift—actively listening, adapting, and creating spaces where fans feel seen and valued—are the ones that will define the future.

Winning Brands isn't just recognized—it's felt. It becomes part of people's lives, identities, and passions. The strongest brands don't chase attention; they cultivate belonging. Put fans at the center, and they will take your brand further than any marketing campaign ever could.

This isn't about a single campaign or moment. It's about creating momentum. The future belongs to those who build fandom.

Built to Last: How Winning Brands Create Legacy Through Connection

Market leaders today don't win by being the loudest—they win by being the most meaningful. The brands that shape culture go beyond selling products; they create emotional resonance, foster communities, and build belief systems that people choose to be part of.

Throughout this book, we've explored the core drivers of winning brands—fandom, emotional connection, storytelling, experience, and community. Each of these elements contributes to something larger: a brand with the power to lead its category, command loyalty, and drive lasting impact.

This isn't just about marketing metrics or short-term gains. It's about building a brand with depth, purpose, and relevance—one that endures. The question now is simple: will you build something transactional, or something timeless?

The Difference Between Noise and Legacy

Anyone can create a viral moment. Anyone can get attention for a day, a week, maybe a month. But the real power is in longevity—in building something so meaningful that people don't just engage with your brand, they live it, breathe it, and make it part of their identity.

The biggest mistake brands make? Chasing short-term wins at the expense of long-term loyalty. They focus on what's trending rather than what's timeless.

The brands that win—the ones that become Winning Brands—understand one simple truth: You don't build a legacy by shouting the loudest. You build it by making people feel something so deeply that they never forget.

Fandom is the Ultimate Competitive Advantage

At the heart of every iconic brand is a devoted community. The strongest companies today aren't just selling products; they're creating cultural movements. Apple didn't just make a phone. Nike didn't just make sneakers. The UFC didn't just sell fights. They built movements that people wanted to be part of.

A strong fandom means:

1. Your audience doesn't just buy from you; they advocate for you.
2. Your brand isn't dependent on paid media; it grows organically.
3. You don't chase them; they **come to you** because they believe in what you stand for.

Play the Long Game

Fandom isn't built overnight. It's built-in consistent moments—in how you show up, in what you create, and in how you make people feel over time. That's the game. And if you're in it to win, then stop thinking about your next campaign, and start thinking about your next decade.

So ask yourself:

- Is my brand designed to last?
- Am I creating something that people will fight to be part of?
- Am I making decisions that build legacy—not just sales?

Because the future doesn't belong to the brands that scream for attention. It belongs to the ones that own a place in people's hearts and minds. You now have everything you need. The strategies. The insights. The mindset. But knowledge is nothing without action. So, what are you going to build? It's time to go make history.